THE COMMANDER'S ANOINTING

McDougal & Associates
Servants of Christ and Stewards of the Mysteries of God

THE COMMANDER'S ANOINTING

BY

APOSTLE L. EDWARD GADDIE

Unless otherwise noted, all Scripture quotations are from the Authorized King James Version of the Bible, public domain. References marked "NLT" are from the New Living Translation of the Bible, copyright © 1996 by Tyndale House Publishers, Inc., Wheaton, Illinois.

THE COMMANDER'S ANOINTING
Copyright © 2007, 2018 — by L. Edward Gaddie
ALL RIGHTS RESERVED

No part of this book may be reproduced or transmitted in any form or by any means, electronic or mechanical, including photocopying, recording, or by any information retrieval system.

Original cover design by Lara York
zoecreationgrafx@bellsouth.net

Published by:

McDougal & Associates
P.O. Box 194
Greenwell Springs, LA 70739-0194
www.thepublishedword.com

McDougal & Associates is dedicated to the spreading of the Gospel of Jesus Christ to as many people as possible in the shortest time possible.

ISBN 978-0-9777053-4-4

Printed on demand in the U.S., the UK and Australia
For Worldwide Distribution

Dedication

To my wife, *Prophetess Pearly Gaddie*. No one could know the trials she has faced with me through the years. Nevertheless, she has remained faithful. I thank God for her. If she had not been willing to stick by me until I came to the place of full surrender to the will of God for my life, I'm not sure what might have happened to me. This day would not have been possible without her determination and dedication. Through everything, she stuck close by my side.

Acknowledgments

I gratefully acknowledge the contribution of *Sister Chrystle Washington*. She did a lot of research for me for this book. When I needed certain information, she took the time to find it for me. Thank you.

I am deeply indebted to the literary skills of *Brother Harold McDougal*. The many books he has labored faithfully to bring to the public have been a blessing and continue to be a blessing to the Body of Christ.

I am also indebted to *my family* and to *my church family*.

Contents

Foreword by Prophetess Pearly Gaddie 9

Introduction 11

1. What Is this "Commander's Anointing" All About? .. 13
2. Natural Commanders 31
3. Spiritual Commanders of Bible Days 49
4. Jesus and the Commander's Anointing 77
5. Spiritual Commanders in Modern Times 99
6. The Seeds of the Commander's Anointing in Me 109
7. The Seeds Grow 129
8. The Seeds Mature 143
9. The Commander's Anointing Today 161
10. What Lies Ahead? 179
    Epilogue 197

    Ministry Page 190

Foreword by Prophetess Pearly Gaddie

When Pastor Gaddie and I started our first church, it amazed me to see a bench full of men, eager to hear every word the pastor spoke and to obey him in any way they could. I was mystified by that. What would make these men react to him in that way? I was the man's wife, and, frankly, I wasn't yet very submissive to him. What would cause grown men to submit to him so willingly? At the time, I didn't understand *The Commander's Anointing*. Now I know the reason behind my husband's commanding presence and the respect he commanded from those men and continues to command from others. It is a special anointing that more of us in the Body of Christ need for this endtime.

Prophetess Pearly Gaddie
Houston, Texas

> *He sent redemption unto his people: he hath COMMANDED his covenant for ever: holy and reverend is his name.*
> Psalm 111:9, Emphasis Added

INTRODUCTION

Joshua spoke to the sun, and it stood still in the sky and stayed there until the battle he was waging could be won. How did he do that?

Elisha spoke to a borrowed ax head that had sunk beneath the water of a stream, and it floated to the surface and was retrieved. How did he do that?

Samson caught three hundred foxes, tied their tails together, lit them and sent them scurrying into the standing corn fields of the enemy Philistines. How did he do that?

Jesus spoke to the winds and waves, and they obeyed Him. How did He do that?

Throughout the Bible and throughout the annals of both ancient and modern history, men (and women) have arisen at critical junctures with amazing ideas and amazing abilities to carry out their ideas. Something made these men and women different from all others, and they, therefore, led their people through difficult times to amazing victories.

Much has been written of men such as Alexander the Great, the Caesars, Napoleon Bonepart, Joan of Arc and others. During World War II, we had people like Prime Minister Winston Churchill and General Dwight Eisenhower, who were somehow chosen to save our world from tyranny. These are men for whom we should be deeply grateful, for without their heroic efforts, ours would be a much different world today.

What was it about these men (and women) that made them different from all others? What was it that turned ordinary people into extraordinary leaders? I'm convinced that it was a touch from God that I have come to call *The Commander's Anointing*.

What is this commander's anointing? How does it work? How can one obtain it? Come with me now, as we explore the hows and whys of this great anointing sent from the throne of God upon those who are willing to become God's chosen instruments to their generation.

And get ready. You may well be the next Alexander, the next Simon Peter or the next Saul of Tarsus.

Apostle L. Edward Gaddie
Huston, Texas

Chapter 1

What Is This "Commander's Anointing" All About?

Thou shalt also decree a thing, and it shall be established unto thee: and the light shall shine upon thy ways.
Job 22:28

If you're wondering what exactly I mean by the term *the commander's anointing*, I'm not surprised. Until a few years ago, I had never heard the term myself. Then the Lord Himself spoke it to me, and I've been learning about it ever since.

To understand this term better, it might help us to break the phrase down and analyze it.

The Commander's anointing

What Is a Commander?

First, what is a commander? According to dictionary.com, the word *commander* can be defined in the following ways:

> A COMMANDER IS ONE WHO COMMANDS, OR EXERCISES AUTHORITY, A CHIEF OFFICER OR LEADER!

A person who commands. A person who exercises authority; chief officer; leader. The commissioned officer in command of a military unit. U.S. Navy, an officer ranking below a captain and above a lieutenant commander. A police officer in charge of a precinct or other unit.

So a commander is one who commands, or exercises authority, a chief officer or leader, someone who is clearly in charge. What, then, makes a commander a commander? Is it the title? Is it, perhaps, what they have accomplished? Or is it something that person possesses that makes him or her suited to that particular position and responsibility?

Think about it. Do you know any person of authority who just got where they are today by wanting that position? I don't think so. A person of authority is in their particular

What Is This "Commander's Anointing" All About?

position for a reason, and usually the reason is that they have proven themselves worthy over a long period of time.

But there's another important element to success in the field of leadership, or command. Leadership is a gift from God. Clearly not everyone is commander material. Some are gifted in this area, and some are not.

Before we pursue this thought further, let us first look at the possible definitions for the word *command,* because, after all, this is what a commander does. He or she commands.

Dictionary.com gives the following definitions for the word *command:*

> To direct with specific authority or prerogative; order: *The captain commanded his men to attack.* To require authoritatively; demand: *She commanded silence.* To have or exercise authority or control over; be master of; have at one's bidding or disposal: *The Pharaoh commanded 10,000 slaves.* To deserve and receive (respect, sympathy, attention, etc.): *He commands much respect for his attitude.* To have authority over and responsibility for (a military or naval unit or installation); be in charge of. To issue an order or orders. To be in charge; have authority. The act of commanding or ordering.

So, when a commander commands, he or she is directing with specific authority, requiring authoritatively, and exercising authority or control over. He does this because he's in charge; he has the authority.

But, again, what gives a commander, or leader, the right, or authority, to do these things? Is it the title he bears? Many might say yes, it *is* the title that gives them this right, but this is backwards. Men or women of authority are given titles because of their gift of leadership, not the other way around. A title is nothing without the gift and authority that go with it.

What Is an Anointing?

According to the *American Heritage Dictionary*, the word *anointing* has the following definitions:

> To apply oil, ointment, or a similar substance to. To put oil on during a religious ceremony as a sign of sanctification or consecration. To choose by or as if by divine intervention.

In its simplest form, to *anoint* simply means to rub oil on someone or some thing. In a religious, or spiritual, sense, oil is a symbol of God's Spirit, and its application through the centuries in religious ceremony has signified the coming of the Holy Spirit to rest upon men and women for a specific purpose. For instance, the priests of the Old Testament had to be anointed for their position:

> *Then shalt thou take the anointing oil, and pour it upon his [Aaron's] head, and anoint him.*   Exodus 29:7

What Is This "Commander's Anointing" All About?

The prophets of old also had to be anointed for their position:

And Elisha the son of Shaphat of Abelmeholah shalt thou anoint to be prophet in thy room.   1 Kings 19:16

The kings of Israel had to be anointed for their position:

Then Samuel took the horn of oil, and anointed him [David] in the midst of his brethren: and the Spirit of the Lord came upon David from that day forward.   1 Samuel 16:13

This verse brings up an important point. Anointing, in biblical days, was never just symbolic (as it has become in many churches today). When Samuel anointed David, *"the Spirit of the Lord came upon David from that day forward."* And that's what biblical anointing is all about. It's never just a ceremonial act. The ceremonial act of anointing was created to help men and women realize what was actually taking place in the Spirit. God's Spirit was being transferred to men to enable them to do some specific task in His name and on His behalf. This was not just a ceremonial act, and the ceremonial act without the real anointing is useless.

The anointing *is* the Holy Ghost, and this was evident even in the life of Jesus, the Son of God, when He was on earth. He became the Christ, the Anointed One, only after the appearance of the dove that landed on Him (the dove being another symbol of the Holy Ghost), and it was also then that miracles began to happen in His ministry.

Putting It All Together

So, let's put these definitions together so that we can understand what the commander's anointing is all about. A *commander* is one who exercises authority or is a leader, one who commands or is in charge. An *anointing* is a transference of God's abilities to a man or woman, to enable them to perform a specific function. In this case, the specific function is to lead or command, to exercise authority, to be in charge. So the commander's anointing is a God-given ability to lead, or exercise authority over others.

This leads us to the question: where did the commander's anointing originate?

Where Did the Commander's Anointing Originate?

Where did this commander's anointing, this gift of leadership, originate? Clearly it came from God Himself. As the Creator of the Universe, Master and Lord of All, He *is* the ultimate authority. He *is* the Commander of all commanders. As much as we might appreciate the authority and power of the great commanders of this world, *their* authority and

What Is This "Commander's Anointing" All About?

power is nothing compared with the authority and power of our God. The Psalmist David sang:

> *Behold, how good and how pleasant it is for brethren to dwell together in unity! It is like the precious ointment upon the head, that ran down upon the beard, even Aaron's beard: that went down to the skirts of his garments; as the dew of Hermon, and as the dew that descended upon the mountains of Zion: for there the* LORD *COMMANDED the blessing, even life for evermore.*
> Psalm 133:1-3, Emphasis Added

> **GOD IS THE COMMANDER OF ALL COMMANDERS!**

God commands, or decrees, a blessing, and it is established, and He is able to do that because He's God. He *is* power. He *is* authority. Therefore, He commands, not out of anger or vengeance (as some might imagine), but out of His great love for His creation. As a loving parent might exercise control over a helpless and needy infant, our God watches over us day and night. His will, and therefore, His commands are for our blessing, our benefit, our good.

As God, He commands, and He doesn't bother to ask your opinion about it. When He speaks to us, usually He gives us no options. It's either His way or else. That's because He's God. He's not one of the boys, whose opinion may or may not be correct. God exists on an entirely different level than men, and therefore He exercises authority over the universe and everything and everyone in it. In turn, everything and everyone in this universe must respond to God's command, just because He's God and He knows what He's doing.

In a family, it is automatically recognized that the parent is the boss. Little children are never given the right to make a decision about what the family will eat for supper or how the family finances will be spent. Those decisions are left to loving and caring parents, and it is hoped that they will have enough maturity to make the best decision for the entire family. What is certain is that they have more wisdom than a child.

In the same way, God exercises a beneficial and caring authority over us. He is our Father, and we are His children, so He makes the decisions, and we do what He tells us to do. This is not tyranny; this is divine grace.

What Is the Purpose of the Anointing?

Before moving on, let's examine more in depth the purpose of the anointing God places upon our lives. God said through Isaiah the prophet:

> *And it shall come to pass in that day, that his burden shall be taken away from off thy shoulder, and his yoke from off thy neck, and the yoke shall be destroyed because of the anointing.* Isaiah 10:27

What Is This "Commander's Anointing" All About?

What was this anointing to do? It was to remove heavy burdens and to destroy unwanted yokes. God's anointing upon the life of any man or woman is a force for good in the world or in the Church. This is why we obey God. He knows what He wants to do to bless others.

God, the Commander of All Commanders, Commands

We're all very familiar with the Ten Commandments. We learned them as children growing up. These commandments, written by the very hand of God upon tablets of stone atop Mount Sinai, were given to the children of Israel as they wandered in the wilderness on their way to the Promised Land, and these ten commands served as a basis for their daily life. They were God-given guidelines for life, and they have been heralded the world over as the most proper foundation for justice and peace among all men.

The Ten Commandments are the most well known commandments on earth, and yet, they represent only a few of God's commands. The Bible is filled with other commands that He issued out of His eternal love for mankind and out of His desire for us to have the very best of everything. God, the Commander of all commanders, issues commands.

The Bible is full of them. The word *commanded* alone is used four hundred and thirty-one times in the King James Version of the Bible, and many other words are used to mean the very same thing. For instance, the Bible

The Commander's anointing

begins with commands from God that brought much of what is into existence. His commands brought about the very creation.

God spoke, and there was light. It didn't just happen. He commanded it to happen, and it happened in response to His command:

> **CREATION IS A RESULT OF THE COMMANDER'S ANOINTING UPON OUR FATHER GOD!**

And God said, Let there be light: and there was light.
                    Genesis 1:3

"*Let there be light.*" It was a command, and when that command was issued, something happened. "*There was light.*" Can you do that? I don't think so. Only a person who has power to issue such a command can do it. Oh, you might say the words, but nothing would happen, because you're not the Creator. Only God has that title because only He has that authority and power. Therefore only He can decree such things and they will happen.

This, then, was the basis for all of creation:

And God said, Let there be a firmament ... and it was so.
                    Genesis 1:6-7

What Is This "Commander's Anointing" All About?

And God said, Let the waters under the heaven be gathered together unto one place, and let the dry land appear: and it was so.   Genesis 1:9

And God said, Let the earth bring forth grass, ... : and it was so.   Genesis 1:11

And God said, Let there be lights in the firmament of the heaven ... : and it was so.   Genesis 1:14-15

And we could go on and on with this. Creation is a result of the commander's anointing upon our Father God. Even the crowning glory of His entire creation, man, came into existence because God commanded it to be so, and it was. So you're here because God destined you to be here. He decreed your very existence.

God's Commanding Ability Transferred To Man

This brings us back to our theme verse. Let's look at a few more verses of the context:

Yea, the Almighty shall be thy defence, and thou shalt have plenty of silver. For then shalt thou have thy delight in the Almighty, and shalt lift up thy face unto God. Thou shalt make thy prayer unto him, and he shall hear thee, and thou shalt pay thy vows. Thou shalt also decree a thing, and it shall be established unto thee: and the light shall shine upon thy ways. When men are cast down, then thou

The Commander's anointing

shalt say, There is lifting up; and he shall save the humble person. He shall deliver the island of the innocent: and it is delivered by the pureness of thine hands. Job 22:25-30

It might be helpful to see this passage in a more modern language translation. Here's what the very same passage says in the New Living Translation, for example:

Then the Almighty himself will be your treasure. He will be your precious silver! Then you will delight yourself in the Almighty and look up to God. You will pray to him, and he will hear you, and you will fulfill your vows to him. Whatever you decide to do will be accomplished, and light will shine on the road ahead of you. If someone is brought low and you say, "Help him up," God will save the downcast. Then even sinners will be rescued by your pure hands. Job 22:25-30, NLT

Now, let's restate our text verse in the two versions:

Thou shalt also decree a thing, and it shall be established unto thee. Job 22:28

Whatever you decide to do will be accomplished. NLT

What does this passage show us? It shows us that God, the ultimate authority and Commander of commanders, has transferred His authority to men. He can decree a thing, and it will come to pass, and now we can decree a thing, and it

What Is This "Commander's Anointing" All About?

will come to pass. He desires a thing and decides to do it, and it is accomplished, and now we can desire a thing and decide to do it, and it will be accomplished. Why? Not because we are anything great. We're just men, creatures of this earth, humans, with all of the accompanying frailties. And yet God has ordained that we humans, we creatures, carry His authority and have His power to decree and command. This is the commander's anointing.

A similar passage is found in the New Testament:

> *(As it is written, I have made thee a father of many nations,) before him whom he believed, even God, who quickeneth the dead, and calleth those things which be not as though they were.*   Romans 4:17

God calls things that don't exist into existence, and He has given us this ability as well. Now we can speak into existence things that have not previously existed. This, again, is the commander's anointing.

Various Levels of Command

There are many levels of command, and men and women move up to those levels as they demonstrate faithfulness and competence in their current position and also a talent, or gifting, to move on to new challenges. Anyone who is in an official position of command or control is a commander, but we also have other titles that indicate rising levels of command.

The Commander's anointing

In the military, for instance, we have official ranks that signify to everyone where a particular officer stands. Even when a man or woman achieves the exalted level of general in the US Army, there are levels of generalship. In modern times, for instance, we've had Colin Powell and Norman Schwarzkopf who were both four-star generals. (More will be said of natural commanders in the next chapter.)

During Word War II, a leader was needed to head up, not only the combined forces of our own country, but also those of all the Allied Forces. There were many existing generals among those forces, but the man who headed them all had to have a special gift to be able to work with them all and to pull them all together. The man chosen for the job was Dwight David Eisenhower, and he was given the title Supreme Allied Commander and the rank of five-star general. We will discuss this courageous and God-fearing man and his gift of command more in the next chapter.

Here in our country, we have a special title for our president. We call him our Commander in Chief. That leaves no doubt about who's in charge. Our founding fathers believed that, even in times of war, our military should be led by an elected official, a civilian. This has enabled us to avoid the constant military coups that many other countries have suffered, but it also places a very heavy burden upon one man. That's why it's so important for us to always elect to the presidency someone who has the commander's anointing. How can a man (or woman) lead us otherwise?

What Is This "Commander's Anointing" All About?

Commanders Are Often Misunderstood

When a man or woman has received authority, or command, other people often don't understand it or them. The religious leaders of Jesus' day asked Him where He got the authority to do the things He did. They knew *they* hadn't given it to Him. They didn't agree with a lot of the things He was doing, but He was doing them anyway. And He never asked their permission. He just acted, like He knew what He was doing and why He was doing it. This fact disturbed them a lot.

In response to their question, Jesus had a question of His own. The conversation went like this:

> **DWIGHT DAVID EISENHOWER, WAS GIVEN THE TITLE SUPREME ALLIED COMMANDER!**

> *And when he was come into the temple, the chief priests and the elders of the people came unto him as he was teaching, and said, By what authority doest thou these things? and who gave thee this authority?*
> *And Jesus answered and said unto them, I also will ask you one thing, which if ye tell me, I in like wise will tell you by what authority I do these things. The baptism of John, whence was it? from heaven, or of men?*
> *And they reasoned with themselves, saying, If we shall say, From heaven; he will say unto us, Why did ye not*

The Commander's anointing

then believe him? But if we shall say, Of men; we fear the people; for all hold John as a prophet. And they answered Jesus, and said, We cannot tell.
And he said unto them, Neither tell I you by what authority I do these things.   Matthew 21:23-27

These men just didn't know who they were dealing with. When the commander's anointing is upon a person, God Himself gives that person a wisdom that others will *"not be able to gainsay nor resist"*:

For I will give you a mouth and wisdom, which all your adversaries shall not be able to gainsay nor resist.
                                                 Luke 21:15

This is where people go wrong. If they come up against you, and you're a man or woman of God, they've more than met their match. God in you weights the balance in your favor.

The story is told of Napoleon one day reviewing his troops, while mounted on his favorite white stallion. The horse became skittish and began acting up. Then, a private stepped forward, reached up and took hold of the horse's bridle and quieted him. "Thank you, Captain," Napoleon said, instantly conveying a new title and authority upon the man for the bold initiative he had taken.

But, as might be expected, this did not sit well with the other officers, and they shunned the former private, now captain, refusing to fraternize with him. When news of this

What Is This "Commander's Anointing" All About?

attitude reached Napoleon, he ordered the man to ride his backup stallion at his side as he reviewed the troops. This broke the resistance of the other officers, and caused them to recognize and honor the newly appointed captain.

In the same way, when God places His favor upon a certain person, men may not like it, but they're powerless to resist. If God does it, it's done.

We will see much more about the commander's anointing in the life of Jesus in Chapter 4 and God's desire to place that same anointing upon you for the future in every chapter of the book. Get ready to serve, for *your* time is coming.

CHAPTER 2

NATURAL COMMANDERS

He removeth kings, and setteth up kings: he giveth wisdom unto the wise, and knowledge to them that know understanding.   Daniel 2:21

Our world has known a lot of great leaders, men and women who had a special gift for leadership and who were able to motivate great numbers of other people to follow them. Because of their special gifts of leadership, or command, these people were able to accomplish great things. A few we might mention here are Alexander the Great, Joan of Arc, Winston Churchill, Mahatma Gandhi, and Napoleon Bonaparte.

The Commander's anointing

A Humble Man Exalted

One of my favorite heroes of modern times is Dwight David "Ike" Eisenhower. Early in life, he made a decision to make the US Army his career, and in 1911 he enrolled in the United States Military Academy at West Point. He was considered to be a great football player, but a knee injury quickly brought his hopes of any future in football to an end.

His first few years of military service were rather uneventful. Then, during World War I, he became third in command of a newly formed tank corps. To his dismay, he was called upon to spend the war years training tank crews on the home front and never saw field combat himself.

By 1925, Eisenhower's leadership abilities were well defined, and he was sent to Command and General Staff College at Fort Leavenworth, Kansas. He was then made a battalion commander at Fort Benning, Georgia.

Then, for some years during the late 1920s and early 1930s, Eisenhower seems to have become discouraged. His career in the Army was stagnating, and many of his friends were resigning and taking higher paying jobs in the business world. What should he do? In the end, Eisenhower chose to stick it out, hoping for better things to come. This was his chosen field, and he would let things run their course. Finally, his breaks began to come one after another.

It must have been discouraging to Eisenhower that for sixteen years he was kept at the rank of Major. It was only in 1936 that he was promoted to Lieutenant Colonel and,

Natural Commanders

in 1941, to Brigadier-General. Although his administrative abilities had been noted, as World War II dawned, he had never yet held an active duty command and was far from being considered as a potential commander of major operations.

After the Japanese attack on Pearl Harbor, Eisenhower was assigned to the General Staff in Washington, where he served until June of 1942. Next, he was appointed Assistant Chief of Staff in charge of Operations Division under General George C. Marshall. It was his close association with Marshall that was to finally bring him to a senior command position. Marshall had seen something special in this man that others had not yet seen. Dwight David Eisenhower was now a wartime commander.

> DURING THE LATE 1920s AND EARLY 1930s, EISENHOWER SEEMS TO HAVE BECOME DISCOURAGED!

Later in 1942 he was appointed Commanding General European Theater of Operations and was based in London. That November he received one more title: Supreme Commander Allied Force of the North African Theater of Operations. In February of 1943, his authority was extended across the Mediterranean basin to include the British 8th Army, commanded by the famous General Bernard Montgomery.

The Commander's anointing

With successes on the battlefield, Eisenhower gained his fourth star. He then oversaw the invasion of Sicily and the invasion of the Italian mainland.

When U.S. and European authorities got together to make decisions about the leadership required for their Allied Forces, they wondered who, among their great military men, could bring everyone together. There were many egos involved.

The consensus was that it should be an American, but they were afraid that General MacArthur would not have enough patience. General Patton, whom they sometimes called "Old Blood and Guts," was a terrible warrior, but they were afraid that he, also, was not capable of working well with others. Whoever filled this position must deal with the giant egos of Winston Churchill, General Patton and General Montgomery. In the end, they all came to the same conclusion: Ike was their man. And just that suddenly, Dwight David Eisenhower jumped over all the others to become Supreme Allied Commander in Europe.

In later years, MacArthur would joke about it: "Eisenhower ...," he would say, "Oh yes, he was the best secretary I ever had." At the time, it surely was no joke.

Why was Ike chosen above so many others? Two reasons are often cited: (1) He was such a humble man that he could work well with others, and (2) He had an uncanny ability to galvanize others and get them to work together. Those of us who know God and His ways know that He had His hand on Ike and had been preparing him for many years for this specific moment.

Natural Commanders

Eisenhower was not just a humble man; he was also a praying man, and he knew that God had blessed him to be in this position of command. He also recognized the seriousness of what he would have to do. He had catapulted over powerful men like General Douglas MacArthur, General Omar Bradley, General George S. Patton and the British General Bernard Montgomery (all great commanders in their own right). When the war had started, he had still been a full-bird colonel, and, as such, he'd had to walk behind the generals. Now that the war was at its height, he was leading them all. It was amazing to have so many great men together at one time, but one man excelled and became the greatest of them all.

Not too long ago, I was at a VA hospital one day and was able to personally speak with some men who had been with Eisenhower in Europe. Just to talk with them was an honor for me.

There are many reasons that Dwight Eisenhower provides us with a good model for natural leadership. When he was later offered the Medal of Honor, he refused it. He had not imperiled his life in the field of battle, as the average soldier had, he said. That speaks volumes about this man. He indeed was a man of integrity.

Dwight David Eisenhower (1890-1969), of course, went on to become our 34th President, serving the nation in this capacity from 1953 to 1961. He was the only general to serve in that office in the twentieth century. In his final days in office, Ike gave a very important speech that has become famous (or infamous, depending

The Commander's anointing

on your point of view). He was concerned that America should remain free, and he warned of forces that could imperil that freedom. He, thus, left us with a warning. Alas, much of what President Eisenhower warned us about that day, what he called "the military-industrial complex," has become part of the American system of doing business.

> **EISENHOWER WAS ALSO A PRAYING MAN!**

Since then, many intellectuals have chosen to make jokes about Ike's predictions, but there's nothing funny about them. What he was concerned about is deadly serious business. America, wake up before it's too late. Heed the words of a man who was anointed to save us from tyranny and lead us on in freedom.

Our First Commander In Chief

Our very first commander in chief, George Washington, was also a praying man. Without God's intervention, he didn't see how this new republic could survive against the might of England. God answered his prayers, and today we're still enjoying the fruits of his gift and of his vision.

We could use that word *vision* in a very literal sense. It's not widely known, but George Washington actually had spiritual visions. This fact has been suppressed by secular historians, who, little by little, have tried to strip God out of every part of American life. But that's dangerous.

Natural Commanders

This is the reason our nation is suffering. Wildfires, hurricanes, floods ... We've had all these things in the past, but nothing on the scale of what we're seeing now. And it's because of sin and rejection of God. This is His way of trying to get our attention. Isaiah warned:

When thy judgments are in the earth, the inhabitants of the world will learn righteousness.   Isaiah 26:9

How sad that we don't seem to learn any other way!

President Theodore "Teddy" Roosevelt once said, "Walk softly, but carry a big stick." That's exactly what God has to do with us. Even animals respect a big stick. Dogs may bark at you, but if you have a big stick in your hand, they'll run. How sad to think that God has to use a stick on us.

As our very first president and, therefore, the Founding Father of our nation, George Washington didn't turn away from God. He did just the opposite. Realizing that we had embarked on a perilous venture, he prayed to God to hold it all together. This new nation, the new kid on the block, had a lot to learn, and only God could teach it. Compared to other nations that were thousands of years old, we were still in our infancy. Even now, our nation has been in existence for only a few hundred years, a very brief span in the course of human history, and yet we're the most blessed nation on the face of the earth. God's hand upon this nation has made all the difference. Washington knew this would be the case.

How interesting it is that today, people from many other nations are just dying to get to the United States. By hook or

The Commander's anointing

by crook, they come to be part of the great American dream. In the meantime, many of us who were born here don't yet fully appreciate what we have. I trust that we will not have to lose it before we learn to appreciate it.

Thank God for the commander's anointing that was upon George Washington, and may God give us more men and women of faith and divine talent to lead us into the future.

JFK and Bill Clinton

Another of my favorite presidents was John F. Kennedy. Since his death, many have tried to use his human frailties to destroy his legacy, but we know that men are men, and men fail. David, whom God called *"a man after His own heart"* (1 Samuel 13:14), was not immune to failure. He failed, and yet God didn't throw *him* away. You can't discount everything good a man does, just because he is, at heart, human. What leader is not human? Look closely enough at even the greatest leaders, and you will find proof of their humanity.

God, in His great mercy, has made provision for our frailties, and we can learn from our mistakes, grow up and do better the next time. But people are cruel, and they will use every possible frailty against you.

Many men (many of them good men) did their best to get President Bill Clinton out of office because of his very public failures. In the end, they were not able to remove him because God had put him there in the first place for a purpose.

Natural Commanders

At the height of the Monica Lewinsky scandal, President Clinton had to appear before the United Nations and give an important speech. As he stepped onto the UN platform that day, every member in the Assembly hall, representatives from every recognized nation in the world, stood and applauded. They were not commending Bill Clinton for his sins, but they were recognizing his leadership ability and the good he had done for this nation and the world. They were honoring Bill Clinton as President of the United States, and that was an important act. The office is an honorable one, having been ordained by God Himself.

When confronted publicly with his wrongdoing, Bill Clinton did something very heroic. He admitted his fault and vowed to do better. And that is an admirable trait in any leader. These two men, JFK and Bill Clinton, with all their frailties, had the commander's anointing for secular leadership.

Joan of Arc, Savior of Her Nation

Many women have played an important role in history. One such woman was Joan of Arc. Joan of Arc (1412–1431) became a national heroine to France. While just a teenager, she received visions from God which told her to recover her homeland from English domination that had lasted for more than a hundred years.

The population of France had been decimated by the black death of the previous century, and now its economy

The Commander's anointing

was in shambles because of the prolonged fighting, most of it on French soil. French merchants were cut off from the rest of the world and could no longer trade, and French troops had not won a major victory in an entire generation. The current King of France, the as-yet-uncrowned Charles VI, seemed helpless to act. He sometimes suffered bouts of insanity and was, therefore, unable to rule.

It took Joan a long time just to reach someone in authority who could give her permission to act. Military leaders scoffed at her ideas, wondering if they had not come from the devil, rather than from God. In the end, she was able to reach the uncrowned king by disguising herself as a man.

After hearing her out, the king agreed to send Joan to the siege at Orléans as part of a relief mission. The strategic location of the city along the Loire River made it the last obstacle to an assault on the remaining French heartland. The fate of the entire kingdom hung on that one battle, and no one was optimistic that the city could withstand the English siege for very long.

Arriving at Orléans, Joan was dismayed to find that none of the officers in charge would take her seriously. They refused to include her in the war councils or to inform her of enemy troop movements. But Joan was not discouraged. She surprised everyone, especially skeptical veteran French commanders, when she was able to lift the siege in only nine days.

Several more swift victories on Joan's part led to Charles VII's coronation at Reims and settled the disputed

Natural Commanders

succession to the French throne. The nation was free, and the people owed it all to this young woman. Those who fought with her considered her to be a skilled tactician and a successful strategist. Her boldness in battle reversed a long-standing reserve and caution on the part of French leaders.

Alas, the rejoicing in France lasted longer than Joan's career. First, she was wounded during an attempt to recapture Paris that autumn. A woman of integrity, she refused to leave the battlefield. That serious wound slowed her down.

Next, she was hampered by court intrigues, and because of it, she was allowed to lead only insignificant troops into battle. Things did not go well for her company at a skirmish near Compiègne the following spring. As her people retreated, she insisted on being the last to leave the battlefield, and she was captured.

> **JOAN OF ARC (1412–1431) BECAME A NATIONAL HEROINE TO FRANCE!**

A politically motivated trial led to Joan's conviction on the charge of heresy (she was convicted for wearing men's clothing), and the English regent, John, Duke of Bedford, ordered her to be burned at the stake. She stood there calling on the name of Jesus until the end.

The Commander's anointing

She had become the heroine of her country at the tender age of seventeen, but now she died at the age of nineteen.

To make sure that Joan of Arc did not rise from the ashes, the men in charge that day burned her body several times, then threw her ashes into the River Sein. Later, her executioner, Geoffroy Therage, stated that he greatly feared to be damned, for he knew that he had just killed a holy woman.

Joan of Arc had come from an obscure village and risen to prominence when she was barely more than a child, and she had done it all as an uneducated peasant. How did she do that? That's the commander's anointing at work.

Some twenty-four years after Joan's death, the Catholic Church reopened her case, and a new finding overturned her original conviction. Her piety to the end impressed everyone, and, instead of a heretic, she was now pronounced a saint.

Joan of Arc has remained an important figure in Western culture. From Napoleon to the present, French politicians of all leanings have invoked her memory. Major writers and composers who have created works about her include Shakespeare, Voltaire, Schiller, Verdi, Tchaikovsky, Twain, Shaw, Brecht and Honegger. Depictions of her continue in film, television and song. What a woman! What a story! To God be all the glory!

Natural Commanders

The Devil's Trophies

At the other end of the spectrum from these great men and women of history, we have the villains of history. High among them stand Hitler, Mao and Stalin. These men also had commanding personalities and gifts of command, and yet they went astray because they had their own agendas. These were selfish and self-serving men, men who were users and abusers. They cared nothing for the people they purported to serve; they only cared about themselves.

When Mussolini of Italy came against a defenseless Emperor Heile Selassie of Ethiopia, the emperor pleaded with some of the other European countries for help. His people were fighting with knives and spears, while the Italian fascists were coming against them with tanks and machine guns. His pleas went unanswered, and he predicted that this evil that had befallen his people would also come upon Europe. His words proved prophetic. Hitler and Mussolini were ruthless partners, and when they later swept through Europe, they destroyed millions of people in their path.

Hitler was the tyrant of tyrants. Even his name is spoken with venom around the world today. It's hard to imagine a man of such evil, and yet he wasn't the first, and he won't be the last.

I had a cartoon clipping from a newspaper. It showed Hitler, Mussolini and Stalin sitting together at a table

The Commander's anointing

playing cards. There was a seat reserved for Generalissimo Francisco Franco of Spain. The next frame showed Franco walking down a path in Hell lined with dead men's bones on either side. In the next frame, the others looked up and said to Franco, "What in Hell kept you?" They had all been waiting for him.

These men were the devil's trophies. They had the potential for good, but they used it, instead, for evil. And that's a choice every gifted man or woman must make.

> **THESE MEN WERE THE DEVIL'S TROPHIES!**

A Forgotten Face

The story is told of the famous artist Michelangelo and his painting of the Lord's Supper. One by one, he sought just the right people to sit for the characters he wished to portray in the painting. The man he chose to portray Jesus Himself was perfect, and he was happy with the result.

When only Judas remained to be painted, however, he found it very difficult to find someone suitable to be a model. No one had a face sufficiently distorted by sin to pose for that infamous character. He kept searching, and eventually he was able to find just the face he had been looking for. This man looked so haggard, so wretched, so miserable that he was perfect for the part, and the man, desperate for money, agreed to sit for the painting.

Natural Commanders

When Michelangelo was nearing the completion of the face of Judas, the man who had sat for it day after day finally spoke up. "You don't know me, do you?"

"Should I?" the painter asked, and what the man told him was shocking.

"Several years ago, I sat for your portrait of Christ," the man said.

Could it be true? It was. In a few short years, the man who possessed such a light-filled face had degenerated so much that he no longer had the same appearance at all. What happens on the inside of us is transferred to the outside. This man had great potential, but he had "blown it" in wasted years of sin, and his body, especially his face, had paid the price. When we have been given a gift, it's our choice how we will use it.

God Even Raises Up Secular Leadership

As we see in Daniel 2:21 and other verses, the Scriptures are clear about God raising up leaders, even when they serve in this purely secular sense. God called Cyrus, a pagan king, *"His anointed,"* because the man fulfilled God's purposes in the earth (Isaiah 45:1). Because of this, New Testament writings warn us about the need to honor and obey secular leadership, showing that it is ordained by God Himself:

> *Render therefore unto Caesar the things which are Caesar's; and unto God the things that are God's.* Matthew 22:21

The Commander's anointing

Let every soul be subject unto the higher powers. For there is no power but of God: the powers that be are ordained of God. Whosoever therefore resisteth the power, resisteth the ordinance of God: and they that resist shall receive to themselves damnation. For rulers are not a terror to good works, but to the evil.

Wilt thou then not be afraid of the power? do that which is good, and thou shalt have praise of the same: for he is the minister of God to thee for good. But if thou do that which is evil, be afraid; for he beareth not the sword in vain: for he is the minister of God, a revenger to execute wrath upon him that doeth evil. Wherefore ye must needs be subject, not only for wrath, but also for conscience sake. For for this cause pay ye tribute also: for they are God's ministers, attending continually upon this very thing. Render therefore to all their dues: tribute to whom tribute is due; custom to whom custom; fear to whom fear; honour to whom honour. Romans 13:1-7

Submitting to spiritual leadership, of course, is even more important. The Scriptures say very clearly to us:

Obey them that have the rule over you, and submit yourselves: for they watch for your souls, as they that must give account, that they may do it with joy, and not with grief: for that is unprofitable for you. Hebrews 13:17

Why should we *"obey"* men and women who are not perfect? Because God has put them into that position for

Natural Commanders

our welfare. They have the commander's anointing. Such men and women have led us to freedom and prosperity in the past, and we must believe for continued grace to have such leaders for the future.

Chapter 3

Spiritual Commanders in Bible Days

And the angel of the Lord appeared unto him [Gideon], and said unto him, The Lord is with thee, thou mighty man of valour.   Judges 6:12

As great as the natural commanders were, they often brought great destruction upon others. To achieve their own personal goals and the goals of their people, they often resorted to cruelty and ruthlessness with those who were different or opposed to them. God's commanders are just the opposite. They touch every area of life and bring blessing to everyone around them. They are called to heal the sick and raise the dead. They perform the miraculous.

The Commander's anointing

They command the heavens, and in so doing, they stand alone in their calling, a calling to do the impossible—to the glory and honor of God Almighty.

In earliest biblical times, there were not yet great nations to be led. Many of the early Bible figures were great in leading a family or a group of families, but the really great leaders, those who demonstrated best the commander's anointing, were to come later, once Israel had reached millions of inhabitants. These were men like Moses and Joshua, Gideon and Samson, Elijah and Elisha. The pages of the Bible are filled with their exploits. Let's look at just a few of them.

> **MOSES WAS THE FIRST GREAT LEADER TO REACH THIS LEVEL OF ANOINTED COMMAND!**

The Commander's Anointing Upon Moses

Moses was the first great leader to reach this level of anointed command, and his life, from the time he yielded himself to the commander's anointing, was one miracle after another. How do you get Pharaoh, the most powerful man on earth, to listen to you and even obey you? How do you get millions of rowdy slaves to follow you into the unknown? How do you settle disputes between family

Spiritual Commanders in Bible Days

members and feed and clothe everyone through forty years in the wilderness with such a large group? How do you deal with enemies along the way, when none of your men are trained in warfare? If you think you have problems, think about what Moses faced every single day.

When Moses and his people faced the Red Sea, its waters parted at his command, and a way was opened for them to cross over. They had been trapped against the sea by the approaching Egyptian army. The Pharaoh was sure he had the Israelites, for there were mountains on both sides of them, he and his army were behind them, and the Red Sea was in front of them. But Pharaoh didn't know God.

The mighty Pharaoh would've had these people before this, but the pillar of cloud that had been leading them every day had moved to their rear and was now serving as a buffer between him and them. All the night before, he had looked for his opening, but it never came. Still, he had been sure he would get them in the morning, and he could hardly wait.

Now the people were escaping him again, and he rushed after them. They must not be allowed to escape. They were a valuable property.

The Israelites were crossing the Red Sea, so Pharaoh attempted to do the same. They were on foot, so surely he could overtake them with his fine chariots, the best in the world. But no sooner had the chariots gotten into the middle of the sea than their wheels began to bog down, and then to come off with the strain. This was not good.

The Commander's anointing

And the worst was yet to come. When the last of the Israelites had passed over safely, God told Moses to stretch out his hands over the sea. He did this, and the sea suddenly closed, drowning the entire Egyptian army. The people of Israel were free and on their way to the Promised Land.

But life along the way would not be easy. One day, they came to a spring that was bitter. What could they do to save the people from dying of thirst? Moses had a solution:

> *And when they came to Marah, they could not drink of the waters of Marah, for they were bitter: therefore the name of it was called Marah. And the people murmured against Moses, saying, What shall we drink? And he cried unto the* LORD*; and the* LORD *showed him a tree, which when he had cast into the waters, the waters were made sweet: there he made for them a statute and an ordinance, and there he proved them.* Exodus 15:23-25

And that is just one small example. Multiply that thousands of times over, and you'll know why these people needed and received so many miracles from God.

In the end, although Moses himself was not able to enter the Promised Land, he got the people to its borders. He did this despite the best efforts of Pharaoh and his armies, despite the best efforts of other enemies along the way and despite the murmurings and complainings and outright rebellion of the people themselves. These people were their own worst enemy, and yet Moses somehow got them to the borders of the Jordan. What a miracle!

Even his own brother and sister turned against him, but Moses went on with God, and insisted on taking them all onward with him. God was ready to wipe them all out and make a new nation from Moses' descendants, but he would not accept that. He had been called to bring these people to the Promised Land, and he would get them there—somehow. He was able to do so, only because of the strong commander's anointing upon his life.

In the end, Moses wasn't able to go into the land, but his successor, Joshua, took the people onward.

The Commander's Anointing Upon Joshua

But Joshua the son of Nun, which standeth before thee, he shall go in thither [to the promised land]: encourage him: for he shall cause Israel to inherit it. Deuteronomy 1:38

Until that moment, Joshua had been known as Moses' minister, or servant. When Moses was about to depart, he gave Joshua a charge, and God told him to lay his hands on Joshua, so that some of His glory might rest on the younger man, and the people would see that there had been a transfer of authority. Moses obeyed. He was to charge Joshua with responsibility:

But charge Joshua, and encourage him, and strengthen him: for he shall go over before this people, and he shall cause them to inherit the land which thou shalt see. Deuteronomy 3:28

The Commander's anointing

Joshua was not the only commander among the Israelites preparing to enter the Promised Land. There were other commanders under him:

> *And it came to pass after three days, that the officers went through the host; and they commanded the people, saying, When ye see the ark of the covenant of the L*ORD *your God, and the priests the Levites bearing it, then ye shall remove from your place, and go after it. Yet there shall be a space between you and it, about two thousand cubits by measure: come not near unto it, that ye may know the way by which ye must go: for ye have not passed this way heretofore.*
> Joshua 3:2-4

These other commanders went among the people and showed them what to do. There was to be a standard bearer, and they must not stay too close to it. If they were to get too close to the standard bearer, all they would be able to see ahead of them was the heads of other people. In order to see the standard bearer well enough, they had to remain well behind it.

For this reason, God has ordained that His leaders always be way ahead of the people they're leading. To lead, you have to stay ahead of all others. You have to be out front.

Very early, Joshua began issuing commands of his own:

> *And Joshua said unto the people, Sanctify yourselves: for tomorrow the L*ORD *will do wonders among you.*
> Joshua 3:5

Spiritual Commanders in Bible Days

God honored everything that Joshua did and said: *On that day the LORD magnified Joshua in the sight of all Israel; and they feared him, as they feared Moses, all the days of his life.* Joshua 4:14

This use of the word *fear* refers to a badge of honor, a respect, not a terror. What God did in Joshua's life assured that he would be respected by the people. Even gold and silver, when it becomes common, becomes cheap. God desires that His servants remain highly respected by those whom they will lead. He does His part to confer that respect, and then we have to do our part, maintaining ourselves above the common and the ordinary, to continue walking in the respect He gives.

Joshua issued commands and saw results:

> **JOSHUA WAS NOT THE ONLY COMMANDER AMONG THE ISRAELITES PREPARING TO ENTER THE PROMISED LAND!**

And the LORD spake unto Joshua, saying, COMMAND the priests that bear the ark of the testimony, that they come up out of Jordan. Joshua therefore COMMANDED the priests, saying, Come ye up out of Jordan. And it came to pass, when the priests that bare the ark of the covenant of

The Commander's anointing

the LORD were come up out of the midst of Jordan, and the soles of the priests' feet were lifted up unto the dry land, that the waters of Jordan returned unto their place, and flowed over all his banks, as they did before.
                    Joshua 4:15-18, Emphasis Added

Verse 10 shows us where Joshua received his commander's anointing:

For the priests which bare the ark stood in the midst of Jordan, until every thing was finished that the LORD COMMANDED Joshua to speak unto the people, according to all that Moses COMMANDED Joshua: and the people hasted and passed over.   Joshua 4:10, Emphasis Added

God was (and still is) a commander, Moses had been a commander, and it was now Joshua's turn to be the commander. And what he said brought results. The moment the feet of the priests touched the water, they stood in a heap. The priests stood in the middle of the Jordan until everyone had passed over. When everyone was safely across, the priests then withdrew, and the moment they did, the waters closed again and went on their natural course. How amazing was that!

We read this story, but do we read it with faith? Just thinking about what God did for Joshua and the people that day makes you want to shout. And that same God has given us the commander's anointing to win our generation for Him.

Spiritual Commanders in Bible Days

After the people had safely crossed Jordan, but before the waters had closed up again, God had another command for Joshua, and Joshua had another command for the people:

> *And it came to pass, when all the people were clean passed over Jordan, that the* L<small>ORD</small> *spake unto Joshua, saying, Take you twelve men out of the people, out of every tribe a man, and COMMAND ye them, saying, Take you hence out of the midst of Jordan, out of the place where the priests' feet stood firm, twelve stones, and ye shall carry them over with you, and leave them in the lodging place, where ye shall lodge this night.* Joshua 4:1-3, Emphasis Added

Joshua called the men he had prepared for this task, and they obeyed him, as did the rest of the people:

> *And the children of Israel did so as Joshua COMMANDED, and took up twelve stones out of the midst of Jordan, as the* L<small>ORD</small> *spake unto Joshua, according to the number of the tribes of the children of Israel, and carried them over with them unto the place where they lodged, and laid them down there.* Joshua 4:8, Emphasis Added

Just as an aside, our God is still in control in the Holy Land. Two weeks before the most recent outbreak of violence occurred there, God revealed it in our church. Then, after it started, God showed my wife that this was just to

The Commander's anointing

be a temporary skirmish. It would not last. Within days, it was over, and peace was declared.

Some day the nations of the north will come down against Israel in a mighty battle, and God Himself will have to intervene. When that occurs, I want to be fighting with Him. I don't want to be down here. Are you on His side?

When Joshua was preparing to take Jericho, he had an unusual experience:

> **OUR GOD IS STILL IN CONTROL IN THE HOLY LAND!**

And it came to pass, when Joshua was by Jericho, that he lifted up his eyes and looked, and, behold, there stood a man over against him with his sword drawn in his hand: and Joshua went unto him, and said unto him, Art thou for us, or for our adversaries?

And he said, Nay; but as captain of the host of the LORD am I now come.

And Joshua fell on his face to the earth, and did worship, and said unto him, What saith my lord unto his servant?

And the captain of the LORD's host said unto Joshua, Loose thy shoe from off thy foot; for the place whereon thou standest is holy. And Joshua did so.   Joshua 5:13-15

Joshua knew, at first glance, that this was no natural man. The person obviously exuded power and authority,

Spiritual Commanders in Bible Days

and so Joshua immediately wanted to know which side he was on. It took a lot of courage, but in this way, he learned that the Man he was speaking with was none other than the Lord Himself, and the Lord gave him the same commission Moses had received: "Remove your shoes, because you're standing on holy ground."

Why do I say that is was the Lord Himself? He was clearly not an angel, because angels never receive worship. John the Revelator encountered an angel and attempted to bow to him and was rebuked:

And I fell at his feet to worship him. And he said unto me, See thou do it not: I am thy fellow-servant, and of thy brethren that have the testimony of Jesus: worship God.
Revelation 19:10

This was the Lord, and now Joshua knew that the very Captain of the Lord's Host would be fighting for him.

In short order, Jericho fell. Those strong walls simply fell down flat so that the men of Israel could easily cross over them. What a miracle that was! The more I read my Bible the more exciting it gets. And there was much more to come.

The miraculous crossing of the Jordan and the taking of Jericho without firing a shot were just the first steps in the conquest of the land. In the days to come, many other miracles took place that reveal the commander's anointing upon Joshua. One of the greatest, to my way of thinking, concerned the stoppage of time.

The Commander's anointing

Joshua was fighting a battle, and he noticed that time was against him. If he could somehow have more time, he realized, things would turn his way. If not, he might suffer a crushing defeat. He knew just what to do:

> *Then spake Joshua to the LORD in the day when the LORD delivered up the Amorites before the children of Israel, and he said in the sight of Israel, Sun, stand thou still upon Gibeon; and thou, Moon, in the valley of Ajalon. And the sun stood still, and the moon stayed, until the people had avenged themselves upon their enemies.*
> *Is not this written in the book of Jasher? So the sun stood still in the midst of heaven, and hasted not to go down about a whole day.*
> *And there was no day like that before it or after it, that the LORD hearkened unto the voice of a man: for the LORD fought for Israel.* Joshua 10:12-14

It's amazing when God hearkens to the voice of a man, and He only does that when the man in question has the commander's anointing. When you have the commander's anointing, you can speak, and God will honor what you say, for you speak on His behalf.

In that moment, the entire universe, set on prescribed paths, had to put itself on hold, until the job was finished. What a wonderful anointing Joshua had! May more of us rise to this level of anointing!

Spiritual Commanders in Bible Days

The Commander's Anointing Upon Gideon

When the men of Israel had gathered to fight with Gideon, a newly called and appointed commander, God told Gideon that he had too many men. Gideon didn't think he had enough, but God said he didn't need any fearful people. "Tell the fearful to go home," the Lord said. Gideon did this, and the result was that twenty-two thousand men packed up and went home that day (see Judges 7:3).

There were about ten thousand men left, but the Lord told Gideon, "They're still too many" (see verse 4). Gideon was to take his men to the water and test them. Those who lapped water like a dog were to be kept, and the rest were to be sent home. Amazingly, only three hundred men were left, after the test, and yet it was God Himself who did this sorting out. He had done it so that they would know that it was He who had given them the victory and not their own ingenuity or strength:

> *And the LORD said unto Gideon, The people that are with thee are too many for me to give the Midianites into their hands, lest Israel vaunt themselves against me, saying, Mine own hand hath saved me.* Judges 7:2

We're still thrilled and amazed today to read of the great victory of Gideon's small band against the mighty Midianites. Gideon went on to serve as the nation's judge for many years.

The Commander's Anointing Upon Samuel and Samson

Samuel became a commander at a very early age. His words were powerful because God stood with him and backed him up in all that he said:

> *And Samuel grew, and the* LORD *was with him, and did let none of his words fall to the ground. And all Israel from Dan even to Beer-sheba knew that Samuel was established to be a prophet of the* LORD.   1 Samuel 3:19-20

How commendable! God protected a boy and caused his every word to come to pass. Samuel went on to have an amazing ministry.

And then there's Samson. For years, I've tried to figure out how he caught those three hundred foxes, set their tails on fire and sent them into the corn fields of the enemy Philistines (Judges 15:4-5). How did he do that?

Single-handedly, he destroyed an army (one thousand of their fighting men)—using only the jaw bone of an ass. He didn't even have a sword to use against them, and yet he won the battle that day against a far superior force (Judges 15:15). How did he do that?

One night, Samson was part of an unauthorized shut-in. The men of the city of Gaza wanted to trap him, so they closed the gates of the city while he was still inside and set up an ambush to capture him the next morning as he was attempting to leave. Not ready to cooperate with their plan, Samson just picked up the gate and took it away with him (Judges 16:2-3).

This was no small gate. It was a city gate, and it had probably taken many men to set it in place. Samson removed it by himself and left it on top of a nearby hill. How did he do that? The exploits of the great men and women of history left everyone wondering.

The Commander's Anointing Upon Elijah

> SAMUEL BECAME A COMMANDER AT A VERY EARLY AGE!

There were so many amazing things about the life of the prophet Elijah that many chapters of the book of First Kings is dedicated to his exploits. Let's look at a few of them.

When a famine was upon the land, God told the prophet to stay along a certain brook. He would send ravens to feed him, and he could drink from the brook. This miracle sustained him, but after a while, for some reason, the ravens stopped coming and the brook he had been drinking from began drying up. This was a crisis. It happened because God now wanted to send His man to meet and bless a certain widow woman.

I heard a preacher once, preaching When the Brook Runs Dry and Crows Don't Fly. His point was that we have to

The Commander's anointing

trust God, no matter what comes our way. He has a purpose in it all.

When everything failed, the prophet knew just what to do. He could have despaired, but instead, he just waited on God. The Scriptures declare:

> *But they that wait upon the* LORD *shall renew their strength; they shall mount up with wings as eagles; they shall run, and not be weary; and they shall walk, and not faint.* Isaiah 40:31

You have to wait, and when you wait, there's a reward, a blessing.

When the brook ran dry and the crows wouldn't fly, Elijah just waited on God, and the Lord told him exactly where to go and what to do:

> *Arise, get thee to Zarephath, which belongeth to Zidon, and dwell there: behold, I have COMMANDED a widow woman there to sustain thee.*
> 1 Kings 17:9, Emphasis Added

This plan couldn't fail, because God had commanded it to happen, but the prophet had to do his part. How he dealt with the widow woman is interesting.

Surprisingly, when the prophet found the woman in question, she didn't seem to know what he was talking about. God can do a thing without us even knowing the details of it. God had set her there to become a blessing to the man of God, and she didn't even know it yet.

Spiritual Commanders in Bible Days

It must have felt a little strange for the prophet to begin making demands on this poor woman, but he knew that God had a plan to bless her. The first thing he asked for was some water, and that was critical because of the drought. People were dying, and here he was asking a poor widow to share her precious water with him. That had to be a sacrifice, but what he asked next was even more shocking.

Next, the prophet asked her to delay feeding herself and her son and to bring him something to eat first. That took a lot of nerve. Because of the drought, she didn't have much at all. She'd been about to use up the last of her meal and oil to bake something for herself and her son. Then, they would join the ranks of the starving. It was to be their last meal. But Elijah prophesied to her the Word of the Lord:

> *For thus saith the* Lord *God of Israel, The barrel of meal shall not waste, neither shall the cruse of oil fail, until the day that the* Lord *sendeth rain upon the earth.*
> 1 Kings 17:14

If this woman was willing to obey the command of a man of God, she would receive a miracle that would save her life and that of her son. She was only required to give one cake, then she could have any number of cakes she needed until the time of rain came again. That was a pretty good bargain, and it came about because of the commander's anointing upon Elijah.

Figuring just two meals a day for the next three years and six months, that was a remarkable return on this woman's

The Commander's anointing

investment. That's what the commander's anointing can do for our lives.

When it was time for the drought to be ended, God sent Elijah to tell King Ahab that his wickedness had caused the lack of rain. In the process, Elijah confronted four hundred and fifty false prophets, whom the king was supporting, revealing their weakness by calling fire down from Heaven and then having them killed.

After that, Ahab was ready to listen, and here's what Elijah told him:

> *Get thee up, eat and drink; for there is a sound of abundance of rain.* 1 Kings 18:41

Of course, no one else saw or heard anything.

Ahab went to eat, and Elijah went to the top of Mt. Carmel to pray. After he had prayed for a while, he sent his servant to see if there were any clouds appearing in the sky. There were none. He went back to prayer. This was repeated seven times. Finally, on the seventh time, the servant noticed a very small cloud in the sky.

That was all Elijah needed. He sent word immediately to Ahab:

> **AHAB WENT TO EAT, AND ELIJAH WENT TO THE TOP OF MT. CARMEL TO PRAY!**

Spiritual Commanders in Bible Days

Prepare thy chariot, and get thee down, that the rain stop thee not.   1 Kings 18:44

Convinced, Ahab rode off toward Jezreel, and as he did, the sky filled with dark clouds, a wind arose and a strong rain began to pelt the land. Then a most amazing thing happened:

And the hand of the LORD was on Elijah; and he girded up his loins, and ran before Ahab to the entrance of Jezreel.
1 Kings 18:46

Ahab had already left in his fine chariot, and Elijah was not even ready yet. It took him some time to get started, but, once he did start, he not only caught up with Ahab's chariot; he passed it by and arrived at Jezreel before the king. How fast was he running? And how did he do that? That's the commander's anointing at work.

One day toward the end of his life, Elijah was confronted by an official military messenger sent by the king to take him captive, or arrest him. His response was startling:

And Elijah answered and said to the captain of fifty, If I be a man of God, then let fire come down from heaven, and consume thee and thy fifty. And there came down fire from heaven, and consumed him and his fifty.
2 Kings 1:10

Wow! That was powerful.

The Commander's anointing

Today, we've advanced far beyond the horse and the sword of Ahab's day. We now have unmanned drones that can find and destroy targets of opportunity. Still, with all of our military sophistication, we cannot approach the accuracy and deadly force displayed by Elijah so long ago. He spoke, and fire came down over those fifty men and devoured them. That's the commander's anointing at work.

Another contingent of fifty men were sent to arrest him, and the very same thing happened to them. When a third group of fifty soldiers were sent to take him, their commanding officer was much wiser than the former two. He had heard what happened to them, and so when approaching Elijah, he bowed his knee to him and asked him politely to accompany him to the king. God told Elijah to go, and he was thus able to deliver a message directly to the king.

What Elijah told the king that day was amazing. He said that because he had consulted with false gods, he would die (verse 16). The next verse tells the story:

> *So he died according to the word of the LORD which Elijah had spoken. And Jehoram reigned in his stead ... because he had no son.*   2 Kings 1:17

That's the commander's anointing at work. It was upon Elijah, and also upon his successor, a younger man with a similar name: Elisha.

Spiritual Commanders in Bible Days

The Commander's Anointing Upon Elisha

God's great commanders did mighty exploits, even defying the laws of gravity. When a young man working with the prophet Elisha lost his ax head in the water and was very sorrowful because it was borrowed, Elisha caused it to come to the surface, or float on the water, so that they could retrieve it and return it to its rightful owner:

So he went with them. And when they came to Jordan, they cut down wood. But as one was felling a beam, the axe head fell into the water: and he cried, and said, Alas, master! for it was borrowed. And the man of God said, Where fell it? And he showed him the place. And he cut down a stick, and cast it in thither; and the iron did swim. Therefore said he, Take it up to thee. And he put out his hand, and took it. 2 Kings 6:4-7

Iron doesn't normally *"swim,"* but when you're a man or woman of God, anything becomes possible.

On another occasion, their food had been accidentally poisoned:

And Elisha came again to Gilgal: and there was a dearth in the land; and the sons of the prophets were sitting before him: and he said unto his servant, Set on the great pot, and seethe pottage for the sons of the prophets. And one went out into the field to gather herbs, and found a wild vine,

The Commander's anointing

and gathered thereof wild gourds his lap full, and came and shred them into the pot of pottage: for they knew them not. So they poured out for the men to eat. And it came to pass, as they were eating of the pottage, that they cried out, and said, O thou man of God, there is death in the pot. And they could not eat thereof.
But he said, Then bring meal. And he cast it into the pot; and he said, Pour out for the people, that they may eat. And there was no harm in the pot.   2 Kings 4:38-41

Did you ever hear of purifying poisoned food by throwing meal into it? No, this wasn't a normal thing. God showed His commander what to do to save the people.

Elisha had that same anointing that Elijah had enjoyed, and he did many great things in his lifetime. In fact, he did twice as many miracles as Elijah, and there's a reason for that.

The Scriptures say of Enoch that he walked with God, and God took him up. Elijah's departure from the earthly scene was much more complicated. He had been sent to choose a successor, and that successor was Elisha. But how powerful that successor was did not depend upon Elijah, but upon Elisha himself. If this young man wanted the commander's anointing that had rested upon his master, he could have it, but he would have to prove that he wanted it badly enough.

When the final moments of his life came, Elijah gave Elisha every opportunity to leave him, and the younger man would not. Why? Earlier, Elijah had asked the younger prophet, "What do you want?"

Spiritual Commanders in Bible Days

"I want a double portion of your spirit," Elisha had answered (2 Kings 2:9).

"You've asked a hard thing," Elijah told the younger man, "but if you see me when I go, you can have it" (verse 10). With that, Elisha made up his mind. He would not leave Elijah for any reason whatsoever.

Over and over again in the coming days, Elijah had reason to go somewhere alone, but Elisha would not agree to it. He was not being disrespectful; he was being persistent. He knew what he needed to do the job before him, and he was determined to have it.

When the two men reached the Jordan, Elijah took off his mantle and, with it, smote the waters. They parted, and the two men crossed over on dry ground.

> **GOD SHOWED HIS COMMANDER WHAT TO DO TO SAVE THE PEOPLE!**

Then, before long, a chariot of fire with horses of fire came down, and Elijah stepped on board. Just that quickly, he began his departure from the earth. When it happened, Elisha was not somewhere hiding his face. He would not take his eyes off of Elijah for any reason.

As Elijah went up, the mantle he had used during his ministry began to fall from him to the ground. Elisha, who was watching every move of the departing prophet, caught

The Commander's anointing

it and put it on himself. Unable to see Elijah and the chariot of fire any longer, he went his way.

Arriving again at the Jordan, Elisha now did exactly what he had seen his predecessor do. Using the mantle, he struck the waters, and as he did, he cried out, *"Where is the Lord God of Elijah?"* (2 Kings 2:14). Immediately the waters parted, and he crossed over on dry ground.

He soon discovered that he was not alone. A group of prophets in training had been watching the entire scene, and they now approached the man of God:

> *And when the sons of the prophets which were to view at Jericho saw him, they said, The spirit of Elijah doth rest on Elisha. And they came to meet him, and bowed themselves to the ground before him.*   2 Kings 2:15

Not everyone was nearly as respectful of the new prophet as these young prophets in training. At Bethel, a group of children came out of the city and began to mock him. He quickly took control of the situation, showing his commanding spirit:

> *And he turned back, and looked on them, and cursed them in the name of the* Lord. *And there came forth two she bears out of the wood, and tare forty and two children of them.*   2 Kings 2:24

That may seem like an extreme reaction to some, but Israel had a new prophet, and he could not afford to be

Spiritual Commanders in Bible Days

mocked. The prosperity of the nation depended upon the people honoring God and His servant. Therefore this extreme measure was required in such a delicate situation.

Those two bears were just as anointed and appointed as the prophet. They had their work to do, and they did it well. Forty-two children died that day.

Now, think about that. How could two bears catch so many children? All those children had to do was to run in different directions, and there was no way two bears could catch them all. The answer is that a miraculous confusion came over the children, to their detriment and to the salvation of the nation of Israel. That's the commander's anointing at work. It does what it has to do in every situation.

One day, the miracle son of the woman known in the Bible simply as the Shunamite got sick in the field and died:

> *And when the child was grown, it fell on a day, that he went out to his father to the reapers. And he said unto his father, My head, my head. And he said to a lad, Carry him to his mother. And when he had taken him, and brought him to his mother, he sat on her knees till noon, and then died.*   2 Kings 4:18-20

These sound like the symptoms of heatstroke, but whatever the cause, the child was now dead. The woman rose up and decided to go immediately to the man of God and ask for his help. She told her servant to *"drive"* and *"slack not"* so that she could arrive as quickly as possible (verse 24).

The Commander's anointing

Elisha saw her coming from a distance and sent his servant out to ask if everything was okay with her. She answered him that all was well and kept going, but when she arrived at the house of Elisha, she fell at his feet in anguish. The servant was about to pull her away, but Elisha, seeing her anguish, told him it was okay.

> **THE CHILD WAS RESTORED TO LIFE AND RETURNED TO HIS MOTHER!**

The woman was distraught and asked why, if God had chosen to give her a child miraculously, He would now take him away from her. That didn't make sense.

Elisha called his servant and told him to take his own staff and hurry to where the child was lying and to lay it upon him. The woman was not satisfied. Why would the man of God not come himself? She insisted ... until he relented and accompanied her.

When they had arrived, Elisha found the dead child stretched out on the bed in the guest room, where he usually stayed when in that part of the country. He extended himself and lay down over the child, placing his hands upon the child's hands, and he prayed. Before long, a miracle of a sort happened: the cold body of the child *"waxed warm"* (verse 34).

They were still a long way from total victory, so Elisha got up and, walking back and forth in the house, prayed some more. Then he was again led to go and stretch himself

Spiritual Commanders in Bible Days

out upon the child's body. This time, the child sneezed seven times and opened his eyes. He was restored to life and returned to his mother.

This is the commander's anointing. It will raise the dead or do whatever else is needed at the moment. It was possessed by godly men and women of old, and more of us need it today—if the Church is to become the powerhouse God intended it to be in this world.

Elisha even exhibited this anointing in death. He lived a full and rich life, and then he died and was buried in a cave. Another young man was killed and, because enemies were approaching, his body was quickly thrown into that same cave. When this was done, an astonishing thing happened:

And Elisha died, and they buried him. And the bands of the Moabites invaded the land at the coming in of the year. And it came to pass, as they were burying a man, that, behold, they spied a band of men; and they cast the man into the sepulchre of Elisha: and when the man was let down, and touched the bones of Elisha, he revived, and stood up on his feet.   2 Kings 13:20-21

This was the commander's anointing, still in effect—even in death.

Moses and Joshua, Gideon, Samuel and Samson, Elijah and Elisha ... they were all great men, and there were many others. Notice, though, that I titled this chapter Spiritual Commanders in Bible Days. Even though Moses and Josh-

The Commander's anointing

ua, Gideon, Samson and Samuel were also political leaders, their leadership was based on their power in the Spirit.

Reading the Old Testament, it might seem to us that no one could surpass the anointing that was upon these great men and women. But the best was yet to come.

Chapter 4

Jesus and the Commander's Anointing

Thou lovest righteousness, and hatest wickedness: therefore God, thy God, hath anointed thee with the oil of gladness above thy fellows.   Psalm 45:7

Jesus was anointed *"above [His] fellows,"* and a great part of that anointing was the commander's anointing. During His lifetime on earth, miracles became such a common occurrence that they actually seemed commonplace, and that's exactly what God wants to do for you and me today. Jesus did not just go about teaching people. He was commanding them, commanding the elements, commanding inanimate objects. And that same anointing is part of our calling today.

The Commander's anointing

Jesus commanded the winds and waves to cease, and there was calm. He commanded blind eyes to open, and the blind could suddenly see. He commanded demons, and they had to obey Him. This was one of the things people most admired about Him:

> *But the men marvelled, saying, What manner of man is this, that even the winds and the sea obey him!*
>
> Matthew 8:27

The miracles Jesus did filled four amazing books, so we can only make a few points here about His great ministry.

The Case of the Boy Possessed of Demons

One day a man brought his son to the disciples for help, but they were unable to help him. He later reported to Jesus:

> *Master, I have brought unto thee my son, which hath a dumb spirit; and wheresoever he taketh him, he teareth him: and he foameth, and gnasheth with his teeth, and pineth away: and I spake to thy disciples that they should cast him out; and they could not.*
>
> Mark 9:17-18

Jesus spoke what might seem like rather harsh words to this man:

Jesus and the Commander's Anointing

He answereth him, and saith, O faithless generation, how long shall I be with you? how long shall I suffer you? bring him unto me.   Mark 9:19

Jesus was primarily disappointed in the disciples. They had now been with Him for quite a while. So what was their problem? They had seen Him use His commander's anointing, so why couldn't they use that same anointing? He was still there with them, and He could deliver the lad, but He wanted to challenge *them* to do it. Someday He would not be there with them, and they would need to exercise their own authority.

> **JESUS COMMANDED THE WINDS AND WAVES TO CEASE, AND THERE WAS CALM!**

In the end, the boy was delivered:

And the spirit cried, and rent him sore, and came out of him: and he was as one dead; insomuch that many said, He is dead. But Jesus took him by the hand, and lifted him up; and he arose.   Mark 9:26-27

The disciples were embarrassed by their failure in this case, and so, later, when they were alone together, they asked Jesus why they had not been able to cast the spirits out. His answer was simple and to the point:

The Commander's anointing

And he said unto them, This kind can come forth by nothing, but by prayer and fasting.   Mark 9:29

The problem was not that they lacked authority to do it. They clearly had that authority. The problem was that this type of authority must be applied through a vessel given to prayer and fasting. When we're walking softly before the Lord, every situation should obey us.

The Case of the Blind Man Who Saw Men As Trees Walking

One day Jesus prayed for a blind man, and the man was not totally or immediately healed:

And he looked up, and said, I see men as trees, walking.
Mark 8:24

I can somehow see this man, disappointed and with his head hanging a little low in despair. His hopes seemed to have been dashed. But Jesus knew just what to do:

After that he put his hands again upon his eyes, and made him look up: and he was restored, and saw every man clearly.   Mark 8:25

Jesus made the man look up, and that brought the desired result. There's no failure in God, so if something isn't working, we must examine our own hearts to see what we've done wrong or failed to do. God never fails to do His part. As long as we're not lifted up in pride and self-glorification, things should work for us.

The Case of the Fig Tree Jesus Cursed

Soon after I was saved, the Lord began to draw my attention to Mark 11, speaking to me about Jesus' attitude toward the fig tree. He wanted some fruit, and because He found none on that tree, He cursed it, and it never again brought forth fruit.

One of my members has a fig tree, and when I look at that tree, I'm amazed by what I see. There are figs in every stage of development. Some are ripe and ready to eat, others are still green, and still others are only now forming. A fig tree should have figs on it, and Jesus expected to find some figs on this one. Instead, there was nothing at all, only leaves. That led to His commanding action:

> *And Jesus answered and said unto it, No man eat fruit of thee hereafter for ever. And his disciples heard it.*
> Mark 11:14

The fact that His disciples heard this is important. At that moment, the full meaning of it didn't sink in for them, but the next day, as they were returning that way, it did. What they saw that day startled them, and Peter pointed it out to the Master:

The Commander's anointing

And in the morning, as they passed by, they saw the fig tree dried up from the roots. And Peter calling to remembrance saith unto him, Master, behold, the fig tree which thou cursedst is withered away. Mark 11:20-21

> **HOW WILL GOD BE GLORIFIED THROUGH WHAT YOU'VE ASKED HIM FOR?**

Jesus had power over creation. He had power over the animal kingdom, He had power over the plant kingdom, and He had power over the heavens. As His commanders in the earth today, God has given us that same power, and we need to start exercising it.

What Jesus said that day should thrill every one of us:

And Jesus answering saith unto them, Have faith in God. For verily I say unto you, That whosoever shall say unto this mountain, Be thou removed, and be thou cast into the sea; and shall not doubt in his heart, but shall believe that those things which he saith shall come to pass; he shall have whatsoever he saith. Therefore I say unto you, What things soever ye desire, when ye pray, believe that ye receive them, and ye shall have them. Mark 11:22-24

"Whosoever" and "what things soever!" That's our promise today.

Jesus and the Commander's Anointing

This doesn't mean that we're to automatically ask the Lord for millions of dollars. If we did, He might ask us, "What do you want it for?" We're not to pray for Cadillacs and mansions. If we did, He would have every right to ask, "What will you do with them?"

How will God be glorified through what you've asked Him for? How will His Kingdom be advanced by what you're seeking? God doesn't give us anything without first knowing how it will benefit His Kingdom. Many fine Christian people want things and pray for things, but their motivation may not always be right.

If the motivation is right, then the answer will be there. Jesus said, "*Ye shall have them.*" That leaves no room for doubt. It's final. It's definite. It's sure—if and when you are asking in the will and purpose of God.

Then Jesus gave us the linchpin that holds it all together:

> *And when ye stand praying, forgive, if ye have aught against any: that your Father also which is in heaven may forgive you your trespasses. But if ye do not forgive, neither will your Father which is in heaven forgive your trespasses.*   Mark 11:25-26

This is a message the Lord has impressed upon me in recent months. I had left something buried in my subconscious for twenty years, and I had to deal with it and get it straight because too much was at stake in God's Kingdom.

The Commander's anointing

A Modern-day Spin-off

Before leaving the thought of the fig tree, I must add a modern-day spin-off. I once heard Pastor Tanner of the Dallas/Fort Worth area tell of wanting to curse a pecan tree. For some reason, the tree had become utterly worthless. It was not producing, and the thought came to him that he, like Jesus, should curse it. But when he went out to do what was in his heart, the Lord spoke to him and told him not to curse the tree. Instead, he was to bless it.

This didn't make much sense to Pastor Tanner, but in obedience, he put his arms around the tree and embraced it like it was a beautiful woman. He then began to speak lovingly and kindly to the tree, telling it what a beautiful tree it was, how he loved it and what luscious pecans it would soon bring forth. Then he left it alone. To his great surprise, when the next fruit season came, that tree produced the most delicious pecans he had ever eaten in his life.

As it was in the ministry of Jesus, cursing something or someone should be a very rare occurrence. We were not born for cursing, but for blessing.

The Cases of the Dead Raised to Life

Jesus raised the dead in three levels of severity. In the first case, the twelve-year-old daughter of a man named Jairus had just died. Ironically, Jairus was with Jesus when the bad news arrived:

Jesus and the Commander's Anointing

While he yet spake, there cometh one from the ruler of the synagogue's house, saying to him, Thy daughter is dead; trouble not the Master.

But when Jesus heard it, he answered him, saying, Fear not: believe only, and she shall be made whole.

And when he came into the house, he suffered no man to go in, save Peter, and James, and John, and the father and the mother of the maiden. And all wept, and bewailed her: but he said, Weep not; she is not dead, but sleepeth.

And they laughed him to scorn, knowing that she was dead.

And he put them all out, and took her by the hand, and called, saying, Maid, arise. And her spirit came again, and she arose straightway: and he commanded to give her meat.

And her parents were astonished: but he charged them that they should tell no man what was done.

Luke 8:49-56

"She's not dead," Jesus said, and "they laughed Him to scorn." He put them all out and spoke directly to the girl, commanding her to arise. She did, and He told someone to give her something to eat.

The next case was the only son of a widow of Nain. He had been dead long enough that the funeral was over, and the family was on its way to the cemetery with his body. But Jesus interrupted the funeral procession:

The Commander's anointing

Now when he came nigh to the gate of the city, behold, there was a dead man carried out, the only son of his mother, and she was a widow: and much people of the city was with her. And when the Lord saw her, he had compassion on her, and said unto her, Weep not.
And he came and touched the bier: and they that bare him stood still. And he said, Young man, I say unto thee, Arise. And he that was dead sat up, and began to speak. And he delivered him to his mother.
And there came a fear on all: and they glorified God, saying, That a great prophet is risen up among us; and, That God hath visited his people. And this rumour of him went forth throughout all Judaea, and throughout all the region round about. Luke 7:12-17

This mother was heartbroken, but Jesus turned her tears into joy. Her son was able to live again because Jesus had the commander's anointing.

In the final case, Jesus received word that His good friend Lazarus was gravely ill. The sisters of Lazarus were sure that when He heard this He would come immediately and heal their brother. After all, Jesus was a frequent guest at their house, and He and His disciples often slept and ate there. For some reason, Jesus chose to delay His departure, and this resulted in Lazarus' death:

Now a certain man was sick, named Lazarus, of Bethany, the town of Mary and her sister Martha. (It was that Mary which anointed the Lord with ointment, and wiped his feet

Jesus and the Commander's Anointing

with her hair, whose brother Lazarus was sick.) Therefore his sisters sent unto him, saying, Lord, behold, he whom thou lovest is sick.

When Jesus heard that, he said, This sickness is not unto death, but for the glory of God, that the Son of God might be glorified thereby. Now Jesus loved Martha, and her sister, and Lazarus. When he had heard therefore that he was sick, he abode two days still in the same place where he was. Then after that saith he to his disciples, Let us go into Judaea again.

John 11:1-7

> **KNOWING THAT LAZARUS HAD DIED MADE THE DISCIPLES WANT TO DIE TOO!**

When He finally decided to go to Bethany, Jesus first told the disciples that Lazarus was sleeping. "Then he's doing well," they answered. "We haven't had much sleep ourselves." In reality, Jesus meant that Lazarus had already died. This was disturbing news for the disciples. They also loved Lazarus, and knowing that he had died made them want to die too:

> *After that he saith unto them, Our friend Lazarus sleepeth; but I go, that I may awake him out of sleep. Then said his*

The Commander's anointing

> *disciples, Lord, if he sleep, he shall do well. Howbeit Jesus spake of his death: but they thought that he had spoken of taking of rest in sleep.*
> *Then said Jesus unto them plainly, Lazarus is dead. And I am glad for your sakes that I was not there, to the intent ye may believe; nevertheless let us go unto him.*
> *Then said Thomas, which is called Didymus, unto his fellow-disciples, Let us also go, that we may die with him.* John 11:11-16

By the time they neared Bethany, Lazarus had already been in the grave for four days, but the official mourning continued. Martha heard that Jesus was coming and went to meet Him in the way. She was not very happy with His delay and told Him so. She and her sister Mary were heartbroken. If Jesus had been there, as He should have been, surely Lazarus would not have died. *"He will live again,"* Jesus assured her:

> *Then when Jesus came, he found that he had lain in the grave four days already. Now Bethany was nigh unto Jerusalem, about fifteen furlongs off: And many of the Jews came to Martha and Mary, to comfort them concerning their brother.*
> *Then Martha, as soon as she heard that Jesus was coming, went and met him: but Mary sat still in the house. Then said Martha unto Jesus, Lord, if thou hadst been here, my brother had not died. But I know, that even now, whatso-*

Jesus and the Commander's Anointing

> *ever thou wilt ask of God, God will give it thee.*
> *Jesus saith unto her, Thy brother shall rise again.*
> *Martha saith unto him, I know that he shall rise again in the resurrection at the last day.*
> *Jesus said unto her, I am the resurrection, and the life: he that believeth in me, though he were dead, yet shall he live: And whosoever liveth and believeth in me shall never die. Believest thou this?* John 11:17-26

Mystified by what Jesus was saying, Martha went off to find her sister Mary, and she was the next to come to Jesus. Understandably, Mary had a similar attitude:

> *Then when Mary was come where Jesus was, and saw him, she fell down at his feet, saying unto him, Lord, if thou hadst been here, my brother had not died.*
> *When Jesus therefore saw her weeping, and the Jews also weeping which came with her, he groaned in the spirit, and was troubled, and said, Where have ye laid him?*
> *They said unto him, Lord, come and see.*
> *Jesus wept.*
> *Then said the Jews, Behold how he loved him! And some of them said, Could not this man, which opened the eyes of the blind, have caused that even this man should not have died?*
> *Jesus therefore again groaning in himself cometh to the grave. It was a cave, and a stone lay upon it.* John 11:32-38

The Commander's anointing

But it wasn't over yet. Jesus was about to do one of His greatest miracles:

Jesus said, Take ye away the stone.
Martha, the sister of him that was dead, saith unto him, Lord, by this time he stinketh: for he hath been dead four days.
Jesus saith unto her, Said I not unto thee, that, if thou wouldest believe, thou shouldest see the glory of God?
Then they took away the stone from the place where the dead was laid. And Jesus lifted up his eyes, and said, Father, I thank thee that thou hast heard me. And I knew that thou hearest me always: but because of the people which stand by I said it, that they may believe that thou hast sent me.
And when he thus had spoken, he cried with a loud voice, Lazarus, come forth. And he that was dead came forth, bound hand and foot with graveclothes: and his face was bound about with a napkin.
Jesus saith unto them, Loose him, and let him go.
Then many of the Jews which came to Mary, and had seen the things which Jesus did, believed on him.

John 11:39-45

> **GOD ALWAYS ALLOWS US TO BE A PART OF WHAT HE'S DOING!**

Jesus and the Commander's Anointing

God always allows us to be a part of what He's doing. He let those who were there that day roll away the stone, but only He had the power to call the dead back to life. This was the commander's anointing.

Jesus' prayer that day in Bethany is interesting. He knew that the Father heard Him; He always did. What He was about to do, He said, was for the sake of those who were standing by as witnesses. They must believe. And then He called Lazarus forth.

Wrapped like a mummy, Lazarus somehow came forth, doing the mummy shuffle. Jesus then called out, *"Loose him, and let him go,"* and when they all saw what was underneath those wrappings, they were astonished. All of Lazarus' flesh had been restored. It was an astonishing miracle.

News of this miracle was very disturbing to the Pharisees. They knew that when a man does miracles like this, soon the whole world will go after him, and they were troubled. Meantime, Mary and Martha were rejoicing with their risen brother.

What Does It All Mean to Us Today?

When considering these great miracles that Jesus did, we must never forget what He promised:

Verily, verily, I say unto you, He that believeth on me, the works that I do shall he do also; and greater works than these shall he do; because I go unto my Father. And whatsoever ye shall ask in my name, that will I do, that

The Commander's anointing

the Father may be glorified in the Son. If ye shall ask any thing in my name, I will do it.   John 14:12-14

That doesn't mean that we necessarily go around interrupting funerals and disturbing graves, but we do what the Father shows us to do, and nothing will be impossible to us.

Jesus didn't stop every funeral procession or call for every dead person to come forth. He moved as He was directed by the Father, and we must do the same. People come to us every day with requests for prayer for this and that. I always answer them, "I will pray that the will of God be done in this case." If God shows us His will, we can declare it and speak it forth, but we can never go against it and hope to prosper.

He is the Source of the commander's anointing, and it is to be used with His guidance and under His specific control. God never fails, so when our prayers fail, we're probably not praying the heart of God.

If Jesus did it, then we can do it too, for the Great Commander has given us His anointing and His authority and power. Also, He has promised to be with us and to work with us, confirming the Word we preach.

We can call forth those things that be not as though they were. If we need something, we can speak it into existence.

Although Jesus is behind everything that is being done, He is now using us to do the work, and with our modern means of communication, we can now reach out and touch millions of people at once. Jesus dealt with many thousands of people in His day, and multitudes

Jesus and the Commander's Anointing

came to Him for help, but now we can actually touch millions.

Wouldn't it be a shame to have that type of exposure and not be anointed? Having the opportunity is not enough. We must be anointed, and the commander's anointing is one that more people need today.

Jesus Passed Along His Ministry to Other Commanders

Jesus was a commander, and He went about training and preparing other commanders, those who would take His place and do His work. He did not choose men as we might. Some of those He chose would not have seemed well qualified to us.

Take Simon Peter for example. I would call him a longshoreman of his day. Jesus went down to the local pier and picked out a rough, crude sailor, and then He took that energy and zeal and channeled it for His Kingdom.

And it worked. Peter, as rough and unpolished as he was, did great things for the Kingdom. Jesus never used His shadow to heal anyone, but Peter did:

> *And believers were the more added to the Lord, multitudes both of men and women.) Insomuch that they brought forth the sick into the streets, and laid them on beds and couches, that at the least the shadow of Peter passing by might overshadow some of them. There came also a multitude out of the cities round about unto Jerusalem,*

The Commander's anointing

bringing sick folks, and them which were vexed with unclean spirits: and they were healed every one.
Acts 5:14-16

Jesus had said that greater works would be done, and there they were.

At the conclusion of Jesus' ministry on earth, before going back to the Father, He appeared to His disciples:

Afterward he appeared unto the eleven as they sat at meat, and upbraided them with their unbelief and hardness of heart, because they believed not them which had seen him after he was risen.

And he said unto them, Go ye into all the world, and preach the gospel to every creature. He that believeth and is baptized shall be saved; but he that believeth not shall be damned.

And these signs shall follow them that believe; In my name shall they cast out devils; they shall speak with new tongues; they shall take up serpents; and if they drink any deadly thing, it shall not hurt them; they shall lay hands on the sick, and they shall recover.

So then after the Lord had spoken unto them, he was received up into heaven, and sat on the right hand of God. And they went forth, and preached every where, the Lord working with them, and confirming the word with signs following. Amen.
Mark 16:14-20

Jesus and the Commander's Anointing

Jesus could no longer be with them in a physical sense, but they now had His authority and were acting in that authority. He was the unseen forced behind all that they did, and the same is true today of those of us who love Him and are anointed to bring His last-day message to the world.

The Commander has gone away, but we have the commander's anointing at our disposal. That means that when we're walking in the will and purpose of God, nothing is impossible to us.

We're not doing the work; He is. We're just the instruments He uses to do His work today. This is the reason Paul's very bold declaration is true:

> *I can do ALL THINGS through Christ which strengtheneth me.*
> Philippians 4:13, Emphasis Added

THE COMMANDER HAS GONE AWAY, BUT WE HAVE THE COMMANDER'S ANOINTING AT OUR DISPOSAL!

Just as long as I walk in consecration and dedication, I can know that all the power of Heaven is behind what I'm doing. We, therefore, need not worry about how we will do things or exactly what we will do. As long as we're walking in the plan and purpose of God for our life, we will bring forth fruit wherever we go.

This was a definite part of Jesus' vision for each of us. He said:

The Commander's anointing

Ye have not chosen me, but I have chosen you, and ordained you, that ye should go and bring forth fruit, and that your fruit should remain: that whatsoever ye shall ask of the Father in my name, he may give it you. John 15:16

Jesus also said:

Nothing shall be impossible unto you. Matthew 17:20

If nothing is impossible to us, we can believe for anything. As we speak and move in God and in the anointing He places upon us, the impossible becomes possible.

When Jesus went back to Heaven, little changed. The miracles continued, but now they were done by the apostles He had prepared.

Miracles cease to occur only when men cease to walk humbly and respectfully before God. When men are lifted up in pride, then the anointing is lifted from them. Otherwise, revival and the miraculous was never intended to come to an end. We were intended to continue doing what Christ was doing, so we should see the same things He saw and the same things the early disciples saw.

The Training Ground

Being with Jesus was a training ground for these disciples. They were in school every day everywhere they accompanied Him. And, just like us, they had a lot to learn. When He told them, *"Beware of the leaven of the*

Jesus and the Commander's Anointing

Pharisees," they thought He was upset because they hadn't brought any bread with them. But He couldn't leave it there. These were the men who would take over when He was gone. They had to learn, and so He took time to teach them:

> *And when his disciples were come to the other side, they had forgotten to take bread. Then Jesus said unto them, Take heed and beware of the leaven of the Pharisees and of the Sadducees.*
> *And they reasoned among themselves, saying, It is because we have taken no bread.*
> *Which when Jesus perceived, he said unto them, O ye of little faith, why reason ye among yourselves, because ye have brought no bread? Do ye not yet understand, neither remember the five loaves of the five thousand, and how many baskets ye took up? Neither the seven loaves of the four thousand, and how many baskets ye took up? How is it that ye do not understand that I spake it not to you concerning bread, that ye should beware of the leaven of the Pharisees and of the Sadducees?*
> *Then understood they how that he bade them not beware of the leaven of bread, but of the doctrine of the Pharisees and of the Sadducees.* Matthew 16:5-12

Revival was never intended to end, but when a new generation dropped the ball and failed to carry the baton, the Lord had to raise up others to take things to a new level. Today, we have great men and women like Joyce Meyer,

The Commander's anointing

Creflo Dollar, T.D. Jakes and others, and these are just the nationally and internationally known leaders among us. In each of our churches, we have some powerful people.

In our own church in Humble, Texas, we have people who have faithfully sat under us and been taught, and they're now very capable of continuing the Lord's work on their own. How about you? Your turn is coming.

Chapter 5

Spiritual Commanders of Modern Times

God, who at sundry times and in divers manners spake in time past unto the fathers by the prophets, hath in these last days spoken unto us by his Son.   Hebrews 1:1-2

During the past hundred years or so, we've been blessed to have the ministries of many great spiritual giants, men and women who had the commander's anointing and used it well. Roberts Liardon in his book *God's Generals* (1996: Tulsa, OK, Albury Publishers), chronicled the lives of some of the greatest: John Alexander Dowie (1847-1907). Maria Woodworth-Etter (1844-1925), Evan Roberts (1878-1951), Charles F. Parham (1873-1929), William J. Seymour

The Commander's anointing

(1870-1922), John G. Lake (1870-1935), Smith Wigglesworth (1859-1947), Aimee Semple McPherson (1890-1944), Kathryn Kuhlman (1907-1976), William Branham (1909-1965), Jack Coe (1918-1957) and A.A. Allen (1911-1970). We might add to this list some powerful and influential modern commanders. We have already mentioned Joyce Meyer, T.D. Jakes and Creflo Dollar. Others include Oral Roberts, Kenneth Hagin, Kenneth Copeland, Benny Hinn and Ruth Heflin. I have another, less well known man, to add to the list.

> I SAW MORE MIRACLES IN ONE AFTERNOON SERVICE THAN I HAD SEEN IN MY ENTIRE LIFE!

The Commander's Anointing Upon G.W. DeLette

For seven or eight years, I was blessed to have as a mentor a man whom I deeply admired. When he died, he was seventy-nine years old, but he was still going strong, and I couldn't keep up with him. I met the man seemingly by accident, but nothing God does is an accident.

Brother DeLette was having a meeting in north Texas in a place called Porter, and I heard that he had a tent for sale. I wanted that tent, so I drove up there to speak with him about it. That trip was destined, because through it, this man became like a spiritual father to me.

When I got there, the service was in progress, and I saw more miracles in one afternoon service than I had seen in my entire life. For instance, he prayed for people with short legs, and I watched them grow out before my eyes.

So many miracles were happening that people were taking time off from work to come to the meetings. Some came on their lunch break. They were being healed and delivered, and when people are being blessed, the minister never has to worry about finances. The finances just take care of themselves. Because of the abuses perpetrated by some ministers and ministries, it hurts others financially, but when people are blessed, that stigma is overcome.

Brother DeLette not only moved in the gift of healing, but also in the area of finances. I had never seen anything like it. At one point, he asked people to take an envelope for some obscure figure like $303.03 or $107.07. If they gave, he told them, before the end of the series of meetings, they would be blessed. And it would happen every time miraculously.

I remember particularly the story of one sister in our church who is in real estate. She took an envelope for $303.03 and believed God for a miracle. One particular house had been on the market for a very long time and was not selling. Because she believed God and proved Him through her offering, she sold that house the very next day. Her commission on the sale was $4,000, but the lady she sold it for was so happy that she gave her

The Commander's anointing

a bonus of $2,000 beyond the normal commission. You cannot out-give God. Brother DeLette proved that every time, and being around him caused my faith to go to new heights.

His ministry was always very uplifting and very joy inspiring. He would call people out of the congregation, then tell them to do something. When they did it, he would say, "You know the Lord told me to give you $20," and he would encourage others to give to them also. Within minutes, serious needs were met, and the people were filled with joy—both those who were receiving and those who were giving. I received more than I can describe just sitting under the ministry of this man.

One night he told us to bring some honey to the service. I went to the store and bought some honey bears. Then, at a certain point in the service, he had people get in line, and as they came forward, he poured honey into their mouths, and God blessed them. The amazing thing was that the honey wasn't running out.

I watched him do this, and I knew that he was not putting just a taste of honey into the people's mouths. He was pouring in a generous amount. And still the honey did not go below the neck of the bear. It was awe inspiring.

Since I bought the honey myself, I knew that there was no trick involved. This was not a gimmick. This was a genuine miracle.

He also did this with soap and with meal, telling the people to bring a bar of soap or a bag of meal, and each time God used the items to perform a miracle.

Spiritual Commanders of Modern Times

One of the sisters from my own church had a rash under her arm and down her side. She washed in some of the soap that had been brought and blessed and came back the next day to report that the affected part of her body was now as normal as any other part.

Later, Brother DeLette was doing a series of meetings in our church, and Sister Gaddie needed a miracle. Doctors had told her that she needed surgery to remove cataracts from her eyes. Her vision had become so bad that she could see only blurry images beyond the front row of pews. Every night of the meetings, she watched as others were healed, wondering when Brother DeLette was going to get around to praying for those with vision problems.

Finally, the last night of the meeting came, and she hadn't yet received her miracle. She was about to go forward, when he said, "Someone here has an eye problem that needs to be healed."

She spoke up and said, "I was wondering when you would get around to me."

He called her to the front and called another sister to lay hands on her. He was moving toward her to lay his own hands on her, when he suddenly stopped and said, "You're already healed. You can go back to your seat."

As she went back to her place that night, Sister Gaddie was laughing, and we all wondered what was so funny. As it turned out, she was laughing for joy because her vision was now crystal clear.

Before, she'd been able to identify someone at the back of the church only as "that person in the blue" or some other such indication. Now, she saw their faces clearly and began to identify them by name. We all knew her situation and knew that we had just witnessed a miracle.

This same gift is now evident in my own life, and another gift: the Lord is enlightening me in the Scriptures, and I can preach now with an insight I never had before. I owe it all to this great commander in the Spirit: G.W. DeLette.

One Mistake Doesn't Ruin a Symphony

I didn't get a chance to know Brother A.A. Allen, but I was blessed to read his books. He was a man of great faith and great miracles. I love the man because I love what God did through him. He blessed our nation.

People are so quick to dismiss a commanding personality or their ministry just because one fault has been discovered. At that point, they forget all the good that was ever done and can only focus on the bad. But how many lives did that person touch? How many were changed through them? One bad note does not spoil a symphony.

I'm so glad that God isn't like people. He doesn't throw us away just for making one bad decision in life. God spoke of his faithfulness to David and what His attitude would be concerning the sins of his sons, particularly Solomon:

> *If his children forsake my law, and walk not in my judgments; if they break my statutes, and keep not my commandments; then will I visit their transgression with the rod, and their iniquity with stripes. Nevertheless my*

lovingkindness will I not utterly take from him, nor suffer my faithfulness to fail. Psalm 89:30-33

God's faithfulness never fails. If there is failure, it's on our part, not His.

None of us is looking for an excuse to fail, but if it should happen at some point in our lives, God won't throw us away. What a blessing that is!

> **GOD DOESN'T THROW US AWAY JUST FOR MAKING ONE BAD DECISION IN LIFE!**

Special Honor for Charles Seymour

I feel the need to give special honor to Charles Seymour. After the great revival at Azusa Street that blessed the whole world, he married, and so many people had a bad opinion of the woman he married that when he visited conventions around the nation, leaders didn't invite him to the platform to speak or to participate in any way. He died very young, at fifty-two, having received very little credit for what he did. He was, in all truth, the very Father of modern Pentecost.

The Scriptures speak of men *"of whom the world was not worthy"* (Hebrews 11:38). God just opened Heaven and welcomed them in early, and that's what He did with William Seymour.

The Commander's anointing

Jesus also died young. Thirty-three years is not much to spend on this earth. That amount of time passes very quickly, as do fifty years.

Seymour was a man of great prayer, and it was through his prayers that the revival at Azusa Street was birthed. Men and women came there from every part of the world to be blessed, and then they carried that blessing back to their respective countries.

That was a holy place, and the property where the revival started should never have been sold. God made it special by what He did there.

But William Seymour never received his just due in this world. I'm sure that God rewarded him in Heaven, but here on earth, because of the times he was living in, he was not honored as he should have been. This was sad, not only for him as a person; it was sad for the nation.

As a nation, we could have had the race issue settled here in America way back in the early part of the twentieth century through the revival that came by way of this Black man at Azusa Street. Instead, the races went their separate ways, and we muddled on for many years in hatred and misunderstanding ... until Dr. Martin Luther King, Jr. came on the scene.

Racism is an ugly thing. Some years ago, I visited a church in Houston where they had posted the names of all the great men and women of God of the twentieth century. John G. Lake was there. A.A. Allen was there. Oral Roberts was there. Aimee Semple McPherson was there. Kathryn Kuhlman was there. Maria Woodworth-Etter was there. William Seymour was there, but he was listed at the very

Spiritual Commanders of Modern Times

last. When I saw that, I knew it had been done on purpose.

If the list had been done in alphabetical order, then Seymour would logically have appeared low on the list, but that was not the case. This was a clear case of prejudice. When you consider the impact of all that William Seymour did for humanity, his treatment has not been equitable in any sense of the word.

As blacks in this nation, we've historically been the last ones hired and the first ones fired. Our jobs have been the dirtiest and the most dangerous, and we've had to live with it. As a result, many have been filled with bitterness and anger, but that accomplishes nothing. When we humble ourselves, submit to our circumstances and wait on the Lord to change them, He never fails us.

There's a great reward and a blessing to be found in waiting on the Lord. Many young Black men have been filled with rage, and it's hard to blame them. But to blame everything on the white man is also not the answer. If we're willing to apply ourselves, we can rise above our circumstances. It may take a little longer for you than for others, and you may have to work a little harder than others, but it will come. You can do it.

A dear friend of mine who is wise and prosperous has said, "We know the hand that has been dealt to us, so we have to go with it. Now that you know the situation, apply yourself. Put in more time. Work harder."

"Now that you know what is needed, stop arguing and fussing about it, and start working to change things. Rise above it all." That's what God is calling us to do today.

The Commander's anointing

As for William Seymour, he was born and raised in poverty in Louisiana. As an adult, he moved to Texas, where he held revivals in many towns. Next, he moved on to Kansas, where he joined Charles Parham in his progressive search for the things of the Spirit. From Kansas, Seymour was led to California, where the Spirit was outpoured at Azusa Street, and the rest is history.

For many years, they had day and night services at Azusa Street, and William Seymour was key to what happened there. When things had cooled a little, and he had time to go and visit the many people he had blessed, and they refused to allow him even a word of greeting in their churches, this was heartbreaking for him. And I'm sure this was the reason he left this world so young. With the recent celebrations of the one hundredth anniversary of Azusa Street, perhaps he finally received more of the credit due him. If not, it will all be made clear in the by-and-by.

Now It's Your Turn

Past history is just that — past. Now, today, we're making present history, and it's up to us what we do with it. And there's always tomorrow. Future history is yet to be made, and you can have your part in it. William Seymour is dead and gone, and it's now our turn.

Chapter 6

The Seeds of the Commander's Anointing in Me

Lo, children are an heritage of the Lord: and the fruit of the womb is his reward.   Psalm 127:3

Can God use the children of broken homes? Can He do something with the lives of those who've had no positive role models to emulate? Can He make something of nothing? Many would say no, but my life proves them wrong. God delights in taking people of low degree and raising them up for His glory, and I'm a prime example.

Broken Lives

I come from a family of eight children in the little town of Sweet Home, Arkansas, but our home was broken up early in my life, the result of alcohol abuse on the part of my parents. My father was an alcoholic, and my mother had begun drinking when she was very small. Her father made mash liquor, and she would sneak into the place where it was stored and drink some of it without his knowledge. That developed in her a longtime habit of drink.

In addition to his drinking, Dad was a womanizer, and Mom finally got tired of it and left him. Then, on top of that, he got sick and had to be hospitalized. That left us children to fend for ourselves. Sometimes an older sister would look in on us, but many times, we were on our own.

At one point, a social worker spoke of breaking us up and letting us out for adoption. We fought to stay together. Family is family—whatever the circumstances.

After our parents broke up, we experienced some very dark times. People talked about us like we were dirt. They didn't imagine we could ever amount to anything.

Experiencing Hunger

We were often hungry. When I see the images of small children with bloated stomachs, I understand exactly what they're experiencing. I went through it. There was plenty of food available; we just couldn't afford to buy much of it for our family.

The Seeds of the Commander's Anointing in Me

After that severe illness, Dad was often unable to work his job in the mill. Consequently, he had no stable income and no way to provide for us. Sometimes we could work and get a little money to eat.

We got some donations of surplus cheese, and that was all we had at times. My father's family would visit us and be moved by our plight, but they were not moved enough to do anything about it. There seemed to be no one to help us.

Eventually we moved over to College Station and my sister looked after us. I've often wondered if we would have survived if it had not been for a man everyone in the neighborhood called Rough Meat. Until recently, I never knew his real name: Spencer Smith.

> **ON TOP OF EVERYTHING ELSE, DAD GOT SICK AND HAD TO BE HOSPITALIZED!**

Rough Meat had an agreement with Kroger's Supermarket to haul away all their out-of-date fruits and vegetables. He wanted them to feed to his hogs, but he also took mercy on us and would pass by our house with his wagon, pulled by two mules, and let us pick out what we thought we could use from the overripe and spoiled fruits and vegetables he carried. Later, he had an old Model T truck, and he continued to pass by our house,

The Commander's anointing

offering us what we could use from his treasure trove of spoiled food.

I think about that man often. Some may not think that what he did was much, but because we were in such desperate need, it was a whole lot—even, possibly, the difference between life and death for us. I honor the memory of that gracious man.

One day, we children were home alone, and all we had to eat was some stale corn bread. Suddenly we spotted someone's rooster wandering by. Whispering an agreed plan, we lured that unsuspecting rooster to our back door with some of that stale corn bread, and then we all pounced on him at once. He never knew what hit him. That rooster tasted mighty good to hungry children, and I never forgot his surprise.

The Influence of the Church

We did go to church as children. In fact, we actually went to two different churches. One Sunday we would go to the Church of God in Christ. Back then, we just called it the "Sanctified Church," and the next Sunday we would go to a Baptist church. We went to the Baptist church because our grandmother on our Daddy's side of the family went there, and we went to the "Sanctified Church" because our mother's people went there. Neither of our parents accompanied us to church, but they knew we should go and, therefore, they sent us.

The Seeds of the Commander's Anointing in Me

The first prayer I remember praying came at about the age of twelve. It was for my brother.

When we were still very small (I was four, and my brother was two), a lady had set him up in a walnut tree. At first, our mother was guarding him, but she looked away for a minute, and when she did, he fell. He was never the same after that. For the next eight years, he cried constantly, had epileptic seizures and suffered terribly. Doctors said that surgical intervention could well cut his life short. He was better off as he was, they said. But that wasn't much comfort to him—or to those of us who had to watch him suffer.

The longer my brother suffered, the more it bothered me. Hearing him crying in the night hurt me deeply because there was absolutely nothing I could do to help him. This led to the first real prayer I ever prayed. It was not a model prayer to be emulated by others, but it was the best a twelve-year-old boy could do under the circumstances.

"They say You're God, and You're able to help people," I prayed. "Well, I want You to help my brother. If You help him—either let him get well or take him (I didn't like the idea of him leaving us, but seeing him go on suffering seemed a far worse prospect)—then I'll serve You." At that young age, of course, I didn't know what serving God was all about, but if God kept His part of the bargain, I intended to keep mine.

Two weeks later, we were leaving for Sunday school one Sunday morning, and our dad said to us, "When you get back, your brother will be gone." I had no idea what he meant by that. Looking back later, I realized that he

The Commander's anointing

> I REMEMBERED WHAT I HAD PRAYED, AND IT CAUSED ME TO THINK LONG AND HARD ABOUT LIFE IN GENERAL AND HOW I INTENDED TO LIVE IT!

had already seen the signs of my brother's impending death. We children had not seen it. What did we know about death?

Sure enough, when we got home that day, our brother had departed this life. God had taken him. I remembered what I had prayed, and it caused me to think long and hard about life in general and how I intended to live it.

About two weeks after that, I had a vision. I saw myself walking down the street of our little town, and I saw Heaven opened before me. I could see Jesus, and around Him were many angels. They were above Him and below Him, to the right of Him and to the left of Him. It was a sight I would never forget.

When I told people in the community about this experience, they had a surprising reaction. "Oh, you're going to be a preacher," they said.

That wasn't something I wanted to hear at the moment. "Oh, no I'm not," I countered. "I don't

The Seeds of the Commander's Anointing in Me

want to be a preacher." Little did I realize that when I had made that vow to God to serve Him, it had meant that I would one day preach His Word, and He always collects on our commitments to Him. Like it or not, my ultimate course in life was already set.

I Find a New Mother

About that same time, another dramatic change came to my life. One day a kind lady in our community, Nancy Spikes, said to me, "Ask your mother if she would allow you to stay with me. I could use some company, and I would help to raise you." She'd never been able to have children of her own, so she had dedicated herself to helping other children, sometimes taking them into her home, and sometimes assisting their parents in any way she could.

Although Mom and Dad were separated, Mom lived nearby, and I saw her sometimes. I went to see her now and asked her what she thought about this proposal. She agreed that this would be best for all concerned. I had found a new mother.

Ms. Spikes cleaned me up, got my straggly hair cut, and got me some new clothes, and then she showed great wisdom by making one of her first good deeds to me the giving of a Bible story book. In that book, I found amazing stories, and she helped me to understand them. There was Samson and his superhuman strength, David and his conquest of the giant Goliath and many others. It was a very cunning way to get me to learn the Bible. Thank God

The Commander's anointing

He used her in that way. I lived with Mother Spikes for the next five years.

Not long after I went to live with her an amazing thing happened. I became seriously ill, and she had to take time off from her work to care for me. After a while that became impossible, and one day she told me she would have to leave me alone and go to work. She prayed that I would be okay by myself.

Amazingly, later that same day, I suddenly became better and was able to get up. As she was coming home from work that evening, I ran up the hill to meet her. God had done a miracle.

It was years later before I thought much about what had happened that day. Mother Spikes had left me at death's door that morning, and that evening, I was there to meet her. God obviously had a plan for my life.

Running from God

Even though it seemed that Heaven had smiled on me, these were not easy years. I would like to report that from the moment I prayed that prayer and received such a dramatic answer and had the vision and found a new mother I kept my vow to God and served Him faithfully. But the truth is just the opposite. I was a growing teenager, and the world around me seemed to be calling me very strongly. From that point, rather than run *to* God, I actually began to run *from* Him.

Before long, I began experimenting with sin: smoking, drinking, cursing and running with the wrong crowd. I

The Seeds of the Commander's Anointing in Me

loved the girls and became a party animal. Wherever the action was, that's where I wanted to be. This left little room for God.

During those early teenager years, I once sought advice from a minister. How could I overcome these sinful urges? I knew that what I was doing was wrong, and I never felt comfortable doing it, but I didn't know how to stop. "Just give yourself to the Lord," the man told me. But that didn't mean much to a teenager bent on having a good time in life.

Today when teenagers ask me, I tell them bluntly, "You have to be celibate. Nothing good can come from being sexually promiscuous. God can fill that void with joy if you'll just obey Him." They're teenagers, and they don't always listen, but many do. The others have to learn the hard way.

I'm so thankful that I never got involved with drugs. Many of my friends who did are dead. God was watching over me. A little later in life, when I was overseas, I had easy access to all of that, but I didn't want it. What a blessing that was!

My commitment to God was never far from me. Occasionally, for no apparent reason, I would become very quiet, and my friends would wonder what was going on inside of me. They knew there was something different about me, but they couldn't understand just what it was. I wasn't about to tell them that I was marked for God. We were having too much "fun" to think about such things.

I went to church with my adopted mother and tried to learn what I could, but my life was in conflict with my faith, and instead of becoming more holy, my involvement in sin

The Commander's anointing

grew gradually worse. This went on until one day, while in high school, I suffered a serious accident.

Some other boys and I turned a car over. That shook up my world. I could see that if I stayed home, I was going to get into more and more trouble. I needed to get away from that community and make a clean break from the life I was living. I decided to quit school and join the military.

My Life in the US Army

I did my basic training and went on to serve at outposts in California and Washington State. In time, I applied for duty in Vietnam. It was wartime there, and that's where most of my Army buddies were being assigned. For some unknown reason, I was turned down. Instead, I was sent to Korea.

My service in Korea was fairly uneventful, except for what happened one night in Seoul: I was riding in a military jeep with my sergeant and his Korean girlfriend, and we had a serious accident. We were on our way to the air base, and he asked me if I wanted to drive (probably so that he could pay more attention to the girl). I said, "No, if we had an accident, you could get into a lot of trouble." He didn't seem to be very happy with that answer.

He went a little further, then suddenly pulled over, lit up a cigarette, and said, "Are you sure you don't want to drive?"

"No," I insisted. So he drove on.

Further on, he ran off onto the right shoulder of the road. Instead of riding it out and turning back onto the road

The Seeds of the Commander's Anointing in Me

gradually, he cut the jeep back too hard, and it flipped over. I suddenly saw the pavement, like an ominous black hand, coming up at me. "Lord, I'm dead," was all I had time to say, and I blacked out with the impact.

When I came to, I and the girl were lying on the other side of the road. My leg felt warm, and I imagined that it had been badly cut. But where was my sergeant? I was soon to find out.

As the vehicle flipped, he had fallen out of it, and the jeep had fallen on top of him. The result was that his head was crushed, and he had died instantly. The girl and I were fine.

I was very close to this sergeant, and so I was so shaken by his death (and my near death) that I vowed to get my life straightened out and to do better. There was a certain hill in Sweet Home where I felt I could meet God, and I vowed to go there just as soon as I got home and to make things right with the Almighty.

> I SUDDENLY SAW THE PAVEMENT, LIKE AN OMINOUS BLACK HAND, COMING UP AT ME!

It wasn't the first time I had made such a commitment, and it wouldn't be the last. Every time trouble came my way, I repented and vowed to follow God. But my flesh was weak, and I always seemed incapable of keeping my

The Commander's anointing

well-intentioned commitments. It was to be no different this time.

When I made that commitment to God alongside the road in Seoul, Korea, I was very sincere. I promised the Lord that I would go to that certain hill, just as soon as I could get back to Sweet Home, and rededicate my life to Him and serve Him as I knew I should. But then, when I finally got back home, there were many parties to attend, and other distractions.

For one thing, the miniskirt had become very popular about then, and the young men in the neighborhood were obsessed with women and fast cars. So, again, I got caught up with all that and didn't do what I had promised. Every time I passed by that hill, I remembered what I had said to God. As much as I tried, I just couldn't shake it.

A Married Man

Before I'd left home for my military service, I had a girlfriend that I wanted very much to marry — Pearly Ragland. But she knew me all too well, and insisted that we wait until I get back from my service abroad. Besides, I was just a lad of seventeen when I enlisted, so what did I know about married life? She also wanted to finish her high school. (I went on to get my GED in the Army.)

After I got back to the States, I was stationed at Ft. Carson, Colorado. I went back to Sweet Home and asked Pearly to marry me. She consented. She graduated from high school in May, and we were married in September. That was thirty-nine years ago.

The Seeds of the Commander's Anointing in Me

We couldn't yet get any permanent housing on the base, so we had to stay in the guest house. It was only to be used for twenty-four hours, so she had to check out every day and check back in for the night. Our refrigerator was the great out-of-doors. That was hard, but we were just happy to be together. Before long, we started our family. Our firstborn was a girl, and we named her Lisa.

Not long after Lisa was born, my time in the military came to an end. I had originally intended to make a career of it, but when my sergeant died in that crash, I lost all interest. He had been my mentor, had taken me under his wing and had taught me what I needed to do to succeed and advance in the Army. He encouraged me to stop spending time with deadheads and be serious about my future. Now that he was gone, my joy in serving was also gone. I served out my original enlistment, and took my leave of the US Army.

We went back to Little Rock, and I found a job with the local Rubber Company plant. It was a good position, and things should have been looking up in my life, but just the opposite seemed to be true.

A Man Under Pressure

I began experiencing severe headaches, sores broke out on my scalp, and I began losing weight. I was afraid to say anything to anyone about it, and I wore a hat to keep it hidden. Then one day, my nephew, who worked in the same plant, said to me, "Uncle, I had a dream about you.

The Commander's anointing

Your head was shaved; you were completely bald." That alarmed me, making me know that what I had was actually a type of cancer. When I picked up a photo of Pearly, Lisa and me together one day and looked at it, I was even more alarmed. The sickness was eating me up, and I was no longer the man she had married only months before.

> I WAS AFRAID TO SAY ANYTHING TO ANYONE ABOUT IT, AND I WORE A HAT TO KEEP IT HIDDEN!

Then my life seemed to really fall apart. I became extremely nervous about what my future would be, and I became edgy and troubled. I didn't realize it at the time, but God was dealing with me.

One day we were driving down the street of our town, and a loud siren went off at one of the local used car lots. There was no reason that should have frightened me so, but the culmination of everything that was happening in my life caused it to seem like something far worse than it really was. It seemed to me to be some alarm signal, when it was really nothing at all.

I was so shaken by the experience that I pulled over to the side of the road. Our car, a Chevy Malibu 396, had a four-speed manual transmission, and I was shaking so

The Seeds of the Commander's Anointing in Me

badly that I could no longer operate the clutch. I had to sit there for a while to calm myself, before we could go on.

Next, I blew up the engine in the car, and, if that were not enough bad news, suddenly Pearly and I were not getting along (maybe because of the way I was living).

One night I went out with my brother and took Lisa with us. When we got back to our apartment, I couldn't get in, and Pearly was taking a shower and didn't hear me knocking. The apartment had a separate key to the entrance, and I didn't have my copy, but I was sure that Pearly was purposely keeping me out.

"Now she's getting smart on me," I said to my brother. "Let's go. I'll leave Lisa here, and she'll open the door for her."

He was thinking more rationally and suggested that it was not a good idea, but I was angry. "She'll let her in. Come on, let's go," I insisted.

Again he begged me not to do it, but my mind was made up, so we left Lisa alone there at the doorstep, crying and praying that her mother would open the door for her. Eventually, Pearly did hear Lisa knocking and let her in.

When I got home later that night, I was ready for the fight I was sure was coming. I felt like I had to do something to get the monkey off of my back, and a good fight just might help. So I barged into the apartment ready for a serious confrontation.

I was startled to find Pearly combing her hair like I wasn't even in the room. She didn't look at me, and she didn't say a word.

The Commander's anointing

I grabbed the child, thinking this would provoke a fight, but still my wife said nothing. What I didn't know was that she had made up her mind to divorce me, and she was as good as gone. All she did that night was ignore me. I went to bed feeling very ashamed of myself, and that night, a strange thing occurred.

At three o'clock in the morning, I was suddenly startled out of my sleep by a voice saying, **"WOE BE UNTO YOU!"** My heart jumped into my throat, and I sat up in bed trembling and sweating. I suddenly thought of all the lies I had told God and my family. Somehow I had to make things right. From that moment on, I would live differently—or I simply wouldn't be able to go on living.

God Was Going to Kill Me

What had frightened me so? I never remembered hearing the word *woe* before that night. I didn't know there was such a word, and I wasn't sure just what it meant. But from the sound of the voice, I knew it wasn't good—whatever it was. I was suddenly terrified, sure that God was going to kill me. Suddenly, I was determined to somehow make it to that hill, four or five miles away, where I could make things right with God.

First I took all the money out of my pockets and placed it on the dresser. If God killed me, my wife and child would need the money. Then, I would set out, hoping against hope to make it to that hill of promise.

The Seeds of the Commander's Anointing in Me

I got dressed, and then I looked out the window, only to find that it had begun to rain. "Oh, my," I thought. "I let all the nice sunshiny days go by and didn't go to that hill, and now I've picked a night like this. How do I get myself into these messes?" But there was no putting it off this time. It had to be done.

I looked long and hard at my wife and child, for I might never see them again. Then, I stepped out into the rain, and as I did, tears were streaming down my cheeks, and I was already praying.

I trudged through the rain, praying and crying. I had to cross a large stream known as Lafourch Creek on a long iron trestle, and as I crossed it, I said to God, "I know now what You're going to do. I'll fall off of this bridge and die, and people will say that I was drunk and accidentally drowned myself. Well, I deserve it."

I was pleasantly surprised when somehow I reached the other side of the bridge safely. But I still had a few miles to go.

I made it to the hill, only to find that it had turned into a mud pile with the rain. I dug and clawed my way to the top of it, and, once there, I began to pray in earnest.

I prayed until there seemed to be no more words to speak, and then I didn't know what else to do. I sat down, rather expecting to see someone coming at any minute. I waited the whole night, and yet no one came, and nothing happened. When morning dawned, I was still sitting there waiting.

It was obvious that no one was coming, so I got up and walked toward the railroad track, about a quarter of a mile away. I intended to follow the tracks back into town.

The Commander's anointing

The wind was blowing and, because I was wet, I felt cold. The sun came up, and I decided to lie down in one particularly sunny spot for a while, hoping to warm myself. Before long, I saw a man I knew approaching. I had dated his sister some. He came toward me and then, without saying a word, went on by. He didn't say, "What are you doing out here?" or some such thing. He just looked at me and kept on going.

Eventually, I made my way back home, pondering what I had experienced that night.

Pearly was working at a mental institution, and when I told her the Lord was talking to me, she was concerned and spoke with the doctors at the institution. "I've seen it before," she said, "and it scares me. Whenever they start saying that the Lord's talking to them, it's not long before they start killing people around them. I may have to commit him before he harms one of us."

"Well, you can't bring him here," they told her. "He's military, so you'll have to take him to Fort Root Military Hospital." She didn't know what to do.

She had reason for concern. I was very agitated, very distressed and quite depressed, trying to figure out what was going on in my life. Everything about my past seemed to be coming to an end. What would my life be like now?

My Dream

That night I had a dream. In the dream, I saw a tornado coming toward me in my yard. I had my dog with me, and I ran across

The Seeds of the Commander's Anointing in Me

the street and hid behind some bushes. But then the storm turned and headed right for me again. A couple blocks from the house, there was a creek. I ran there next, and, finding some bushes, I hid behind them.

I never knew where the knife came from, but suddenly I had a knife in my hand, and I was saying, "If it comes over here, I'm going to kill it."

I was talking in my sleep, and I woke Pearly up. Overhearing what I was saying, she began to try to shake me awake. As she did, I kept shouting, "I'm not going to kill it! I'm not going to kill it! I'm not going to kill it!" Even as she woke me up, she worried that I had already lost my mind.

It was three o'clock again, and I got up, covered in a cold sweat. I dressed, went outside, and started walking toward College Station. Before long, my attention was drawn to a powerful star that stood out in the

I PRAYED UNTIL THERE SEEMED TO BE NO MORE WORDS TO SPEAK!

night sky. I hadn't noticed that particular star before. It seemed oddly out of place. God was speaking to me again.

"Okay, Lord," I said. "I surrender. I will do what You want me to do." Somehow I knew that I would never have peace until I finally did surrender. It was not long after that when I met a pastor working in the same plant. It was the God connection that would lead to my transformation.

Chapter 7

The Seeds Grow

But other fell into good ground, and brought forth fruit, some an hundredfold, some sixtyfold, some thirtyfold. Who hath ears to hear, let him hear. Matthew 13:8-9

Eventually, I became convinced that God had placed Pastor Arthur Devine at the plant just for me, but when he first invited me to church, I put him off—as was my custom. Thank God he was persistent and didn't give up on me.

One day, I was out playing basketball with some friends up the block from our apartment, and the pastor came and stood to the side, waiting for me to finish, so that we could talk. I tried to ignore him, hoping that he would go away. Then, something happened that really got my attention.

The Commander's anointing

I went for the ball and, in doing so, I brushed up against another player. His clothing rubbed my open eye and irritated it severely. The next morning, the eye was filled with green ooze. I knew that God was tapping me on the shoulder and saying to me, "Come on. I'm tired of your foolishness. It's time to yield yourself to Me."

"Okay, Lord," I prayed. "I'm going to the doctor, but I will obey You, and I will go to church." The next morning, my eye was completely healed. The Lord was doing whatever it took to get me to come on in, and this time, I was more cooperative.

> **THE NEXT MORNING, MY EYE WAS COMPLETELY HEALED!**

I Was Saved

Pastor Devine's church was not exactly what I had been accustomed to attending. Most churches I had gone to were just like social events. There was no challenge. But this church was different. It was another congregation of the Church of God in Christ, a Spirit-filled and Spirit-anointed church. The people worshipped, and they prayed. I loved it, and I went every night.

I enjoyed attending the church, but it was only when I attended a youth congress in Pine Bluff that the Lord began to deal with me very seriously. When I would get back home at night, Pearly would ask me, "Did you get the Spirit tonight?"

The Seeds Grow

"No," I would have to admit. I hated her asking, but at the same time, I knew that my old life was over. It was my time to join the Kingdom.

I was saved on Memorial Day in 1970. Not long afterward, the Lord filled me with the Holy Ghost, and then my whole life really changed. The next day, as I was working at my machine in the plant, a great light shone around me. It was not just light; it was the presence of the Lord, shining down on me like a floodlight. I sensed that I should look up, but somehow I didn't. Today I wonder what might have happened if I had. It was a great opportunity that I missed. I went outside, totally disgusted with myself for not having done what I knew I should have in that moment.

Once I surrendered to the Lord, the sores on my head dried up, the scabs fell off, and I was completely healed.

Pearly Joined Me in the Kingdom

To this point, Pearly wasn't showing much interest in the church. One evening, the pastor came to the house to visit us and, hearing his name, she said to him, "So your name's Divine. Are you any kin to that Father Divine in Philadelphia?" (The infamous Father Divine operated a very well known false cult in that city at the time.)

"No," he answered, "our name is spelled with an e, D-e-v-i-n-e."

"Oh," she said, hardly convinced. "Well, why don't you go on to the back room and leave us alone [she had a neighbor friend there with her]. Lee's back there."

The Commander's anointing

Later the pastor was heard to say, "This man may find God's ways, but I'm not sure about his wife. She's something else."

But not too long after I was saved, Pearly told her friends, "My old man got saved, and he's going to church and trying to live right. I guess I'd better go over there and find out what's going on." She was expecting our second child at the time.

The first night Pearly went to church with me, Pastor preached a sermon from the following text:

> *Wherefore seeing we also are compassed about with so great a cloud of witnesses, let us lay aside every weight, and the sin which doth so easily beset us, and let us run with patience the race that is set before us, looking unto Jesus the author and finisher of our faith; who for the joy that was set before him endured the cross, despising the shame, and is set down at the right hand of the throne of God.*   Hebrews 12:1-2

His sermon that night was entitled Lay It Aside and Run, and it captivated Pearly. It seemed to her that every word was directed to her personally, and she forgot all about me beside her and concentrated on what God was saying through the pastor. The Lord was stripping away everything from her former life and laying bare her soul. She was saved that very night.

The night she was filled with the Spirit, she began speaking in tongues a little right in her seat. Then, the Spirit

The Seeds Grow

seemed to pull her from her seat and lead her to the front, where she was gloriously baptized in the Holy Ghost.

Pearly's conversion had a domino affect on her family. Soon, her twin sister was saved and *her* husband, then another sister and *her* husband, until a whole new congregation came in with us. Some of them are pastoring today and doing a great work for God.

A visiting missionary, seeing the large group of us who had come in at about the same time, said to us all, "You represent the next move of God." We laid claimed to that word.

I Was Called to Pastor

One day the Lord showed me a vision. I was in a big field, and I was using a hoe, chopping weeds. I sensed that it was time to get out into ministry. That next week my brother-in-law and I went to a nearby town called Hensley, looking for an opportunity to preach in the streets there. Stopping at a local club, we asked the owner if we could hook our electric chord to his system, so that we could hold a street meeting. He didn't want to let us do that, but my brother-in-law is stubborn, and doesn't give up easily. Eventually the man relented, and we held our meeting. That night the daughter of the club owner got saved.

A Baptist lady approached me and asked if she could get the Holy Ghost. I assured her that she could. The result was that we started a daily street service in her yard. At times, cars were lined up on both sides of the street with people in them listening, and some people came with their lawn

The Commander's anointing

chairs, so they could enjoy the service. I preached for an entire week there, and at the end of the week, twenty-six souls had been saved.

I was wondering what to do next, and when I asked my pastor, he said, "It's too far for you to try to bring them here to our services. You're going to have to start a work there." During the next service in the yard in Hensley, I told the people about our intentions to start a church. After the service, a young man approached me and said, "There's an old building down that way [pointing] that has been used sometimes for services. You could probably get it."

I went with him to see the building. It wasn't much. The roof had a serious sway in it, like a broke-back mule, and the floors were rather rotted. The young man said he could help to put it into better shape, so I reluctantly agreed.

We Opened Our First Church

There was another building in town that I liked better. It was a store front, but a Methodist preacher had bought it and was fixing it up to use as a community church. "He's fixing that up for me," I told Sister Gaddie. "That's the building I'm going to have." Sure enough, the Methodist man never used the building, so he rented it to us, and that's where we started our first church.

We were away from any outside influences, and that was good. God sent some old saints, who came and mentored us. It was wonderful. They fasted and prayed with us and

The Seeds Grow

helped us in many ways, and in that place, we saw God do many wonderful miracles.

Still, I wasn't happy with what we had. I looked around at what other churches had and what we didn't have, and I complained. We didn't have nice pews. We didn't have fancy musical instruments. Overhearing me talking like that, those older saints spoke with great wisdom. "Brother Gaddie, you don't know what you have here. Those natural things are nice, but you have the moving of the Spirit." It was true. Other churches, hearing about the moving of the Spirit in that place, were sending their difficult cases to us, so that we could help them be delivered.

> "HE'S FIXING THAT UP FOR ME," I TOLD SISTER GADDIE!

Severe Persecution

In time, with the move of God, came severe persecution. At first, the people just let the air out of our tires and ran into the light pole during our service, trying to cut our power off in the middle of everything. Then, gradually, it became more serious. They caught one of our brothers outside alone and put a knife to his throat, threatening him.

When I was praying about this one day, the Lord said to me, "Go out into the surrounding community and minister."

The Commander's anointing

"But they hate us," I protested. I couldn't imagine what good we could accomplish by doing that. The Lord insisted, so I went anyway.

Sure enough, the people talked bad to us everywhere we went. But then, God did something very unusual.

An older gentleman, an evangelist, had begun attending our services, and now he came prayed up and ready to speak a word to the town. When we arrived for the service, everyone was there waiting. This man was out in the street, and he was doing something we had never seen before. He was prophesying against the community that was treating us so badly. His words were powerful and, as he gave them, he turned to the four corners of the earth. We felt that this was God's timing and His notice for us to leave that place, so we closed the church, ready to move on to other, more hospitable, soil.

After we had left that town, all Hell seemed to break loose there. Murders were committed, fires broke out, and anything that could happen did happen. The next time we saw people from that community, they begged us to come back. "We can't," we told them. "The Lord told us to go, but we're happy that He gave us the opportunity to minister to you during those years."

Our Move to Wrightsville

Next, the Lord told us to go to Wrightsville, about six miles up the road from Hensley. There we found a little shotgun building. It couldn't have been much larger than

The Seeds Grow

15 X 30 or, at the most, 35. The owner, the daughter of a man who had pastored there in former years, agreed to rent it to us. Oh, how the glory of God would come down in that place!

We had so many preachers come there. Sometimes it was like having a barnyard full of roosters. Those were great times in God!

We didn't know to call what was happening a revival, but now we know that's what it was. I felt sorry for some of our most loyal people. They got so weary from attending every night. "If you need to stay home and rest some, I'll understand," I told them. "But I can't close the place. Too many people are coming to be blessed."

People were coming from every direction. We didn't know them, and they didn't know us, but God was bringing them in to get saved, be healed or experience some other miracle, and also to be baptized in the Holy Ghost.

Our daughter Lisa was filled with the Holy Ghost during those meetings. We had never seen anything quite like it. Her mouth was red like fire, and her tongue was completely out of her mouth, and still she was able to speak in tongues.

One night, there were so many people in that little building, and they were rejoicing so much that the building, which sat on blocks, was literally bouncing up and down. I went outside to see what was happening and was so alarmed that I had to pray: "God, please don't let this building collapse with these people inside." It didn't.

The Commander's anointing

During those meetings, a Spirit-filled lady, Sister Williams, began singing to me in prophecy. "Elder Gaddie," she sang, "the Lord will build you a church soon." There was more to the prophecy, but we welcomed that part. We desperately needed more space. The little building was full to capacity.

The next day I set out to find a larger building. About a mile up on the left was a block building. It had once been a Baptist Mission Church, but no one had been using it for a while. We secured it from the Baptists, moved our people there, and the revival continued and expanded until that building, too, was filled.

> **THE DRIVER SWERVED AND HIT US IN THE REAR, AND OUR VAN WENT FLYING!**

I Was Called to Full-Time Service

While we were in Wrightsville, I began to sense that God was calling me to leave my job and go into full-time service. This was hard for me because I was earning well. I didn't like the idea of placing my financial future in the hands of other people, and in my opinion, that's what I would be doing. It never occurred to me that I would be placing my financial future in the hands of God.

The Seeds Grow

Pearly had a dream, and she saw my back full of stripes. I thought I knew what that meant, and I didn't dare say no to God, but I did the same by just continuing on as I was. Two things happened to show me that it was time to make the move to full-time ministry.

First, we were hit in a freak accident. One day, as we were on our way home from a grocery store, we came upon a scene of violence. A car was approaching at high speed, and policemen were crouching in a firing position, ready to fire at the man driving. We learned later that the man had been writing bad checks, but the police had misunderstood and thought that he had just robbed a bank. This was the reason the situation had escalated into something so serious so quickly.

The police fired, and the windshield of the speeding vehicle shattered. The driver swerved and hit us in the rear, and our van went flying.

In that moment, I felt death in the air, and when we landed, I was more than a little shook up. My neck felt stiff, and I limped for many days, bruised and battered by the experience. I had to take a week off from work.

Then an even more serious accident occurred. Until that day, every time I had gone into work at 7:00 each morning at the plant, my machine was already in operation from the previous shift. This time, someone had missed that shift, and the machine was turned off.

This machine had some very serious sharp blades on it. At a certain point in the process of making a truck inner tube, those blades came up and cut off the excess rubber.

The Commander's anointing

What I didn't know was that when the machine started, those blades would come up quickly, and I had my right hand in the way when they did.

The blade sliced across the top of my wrist, blood shot up, and all five of my fingers on that hand instantly fell limp. The ligaments leading to them had been severed. I felt the presence of the Lord standing there, and I said, "I'm sorry, Lord. You're right." In that moment, I totally surrendered in my heart to do what the Lord wanted me to do.

To get the ligaments sown back, the doctor had to cut my hand open even more. He was able to tie everything back together, and I had to go through a long period of healing and rehabilitation. But I did eventually regain full use of the hand.

Looking back now, I understand it all, but at the time, it was not nearly as clear. God had a great future for us, and we needed to take steps toward that future.

The Move to North Little Rock

After we had been in Wrightsville for a while and encountered such great success with the church, we decided to move it into North Little Rock. We found a building there that would seat about fifteen hundred. The owners agreed to lease it to us with an option to buy, and we moved our people there.

It was in that place that I learned a very hard lesson: bigger is not always better. Before long, it seemed to me that our people no longer had the same zeal as before. Somehow they had become complacent, and that was discouraging. I prayed fervently, telling God that He could continue to move—even when the people were not moving with Him. But, of course, I was wrong. God can't go beyond our will to move with Him.

Long before the people of Israel had approached the Promised Land, Joshua had declared, "We are able to go up and take the country" (Numbers 13:30). But because others brought a contrary report, the entire nation had been prevented from entering in. This is what happened to us now. It was with a very heavy heart that we closed the church in North Little Rock.

On to Houston, Texas

God had told us that we would be moving to another city—exactly where we didn't yet know. I began doing evangelistic work, and joined ranks with Bishop James McNeil, Jr. who asked me to be part of his National Christian Fellowship. I eventually became Vice President of the organization, and we were called upon to help open new fields around the country. This was what first led me to Houston, Texas.

I liked the city, and it seemed to like me. As the Lord opened doors, I ministered revivals in Latino churches, white churches and black churches. One day I called Pearly and told her that I loved the place and would like to move there eventually. She prayed, and two prophets, one from the East Coast and one from

The Commander's anointing

the West, called to tell her that this was the will of God. They hadn't known that I was, even then, in Houston in revival meetings.

It seemed very strange to me that anywhere I had ever gone away from home, I always looked forward to getting back just as quickly as possible. This time, however, I felt a serious desire to stay right where I was. God was setting us up for ministry in Houston. Within a year, we were living there permanently. It was 1984.

We didn't start a church in Houston immediately. For the first several years, we worked as evangelists, conducting meetings from church to church. The bad experience in North Little Rock had soured me somewhat on the pastorate, and I thought I would be just as happy as an evangelist the rest of my life.

In time, a blind evangelist prophesied to us that it was time to start a church, and our Houston congregation was born. Our first church in Hensley, later moved to Wrightsville and then North Little Rock, had been called Whole Truth Temple Church of God in Christ. This church we called simply Whole Truth Church. Before long, another elderly prophet came along and said, "This is not just Whole Truth Church; it's New Jerusalem Whole Truth Church." We officially changed the name of the church.

That has been many years ago. Today, we own a fine piece of land and are preparing to construct on it the buildings God has laid upon our hearts for the ministries of the future.

Chapter 8

THE SEEDS MATURE

And the sons of the prophets said unto Elisha, Behold now, the place where we dwell with thee is too strait for us. Let us go, we pray thee, unto Jordan, and take thence every man a beam, and let us make us a place there, where we may dwell.   2 Kings 6:1-2

The commander's anointing did not develop in me overnight. It was a growing process, and God used various people to bring it about.

My Pastor Recognized My Gift

When I met Pastor Devine in the tire and rubber plant, he quickly took me under his wing, recognizing that I was

The Commander's anointing

called to leadership. In the Army, I had made the rank of sergeant without ever having studied for it formally. I did read some books, but I was never required to go before a review board. All I can say is that my superiors saw something in me that merited this special treatment.

Before I became a sergeant (while stationed at Ft. Carson, Colorado), I was still a Specialist 4th class, but I was already doing the work of a sergeant, operating as a platoon leader, which is equivalent to a Sergeant E5. I was Sergeant of the Guard. I was told by a superior, "Your promotion has already been approved, and when you get back from leave, your sergeant's stripe will be here waiting for you." Sure enough, by the time I got back, my stripe was ready. My pastor was able to see that same anointing in me years later, and it led to my rapid advancement in the church.

In our church, it was customary for a promising man to first become a deacon. Then, if he continued to prove himself faithful, he could be promoted to other ministries. Pastor Devine bypassed the deacon stage in my case and thrust me right into ministry. "I want you to be the assistant to my Sunday school superintendent," he told me. The superintendent was an elderly lady, and when she went on to be with the Lord, I became the new superintendent.

It never seemed strange to me that I had been elevated so quickly. I knew that I was supposed to be where I was. God had ordained it. There was much more to come. In the meantime, I was learning and gaining experience.

Our pastor was an avid outdoorsman, and he loved to conduct tent revivals and street meetings. One day I was

The Seeds Mature

out with him in some street services, and he said, "Would you like to testify?"

"Sure," I answered, and he gave me the opportunity.

While I was testifying, I felt something happen. A preaching anointing came over me. I knew that was not what I had been asked to do, so I looked to the pastor for guidance. "Go ahead," he said, delighted to see this anointing upon my life. And that's how I got started preaching.

My first official sermon was preached at Rush Island in North Little Rock. It was based on 2 Kings 6, our text verse for this chapter. My message that day was, "The Way Is NOT *'Too Strait.'*"

I worked with Pastor Devine in many revivals. It was not unusual for us to travel a hundred miles or more one way to preach somewhere, then turn around and travel back that night after the service. In this way, I stayed under the tent and in street services a great part of the time. This man imparted the evangelistic spirit to me and my wife, and this same thing has happened to our people today. They've caught the zeal of the soulwinner.

> **PASTOR DEVINE BYPASSED THE DEACON STAGE IN MY CASE AND THRUST ME RIGHT INTO MINISTRY!**

The Commander's anointing

I Was Ordained

After I preached that first time, the state meetings of the Church of God in Christ were coming up, and Pastor said to me, "I expect you to be there every night." I didn't fail. He wasn't able to be there every night himself, but he always had someone to let him know if I was there or not. He was testing me, preparing me for advancement.

When he was sufficiently satisfied that I was able to be a faithful follower under him, he told me that I was being sent before the Elders' Council to be ordained. I'd had no idea that this was coming. It happened very suddenly.

"Why do you want to be ordained?" one council member asked me. "Will having papers help you do your ministry?"

"I don't really need papers to do what I'm doing," I answered, "but because I've been placed over other people, it seems only right that I be ordained. Also, I think it's a matter of maintaining legality before the state, especially in the case of having to conduct a marriage."

They continued to ask me questions, and I later realized that I needed to hear these particular questions. Another of their questions was this: "If your wife, at some point, should be overcome with temptation, and slept with another man, what would you do?"

"I'd divorce her," I told them frankly.

They didn't like that answer. "Do you mean to tell us you're a Holy Ghost filled preacher, and this is what you're

The Seeds Mature

going to be ministering to your people: when things get tough in your marriage, just divorce your spouse?"

"Well, the Scriptures make allowance for that," I insisted. "If a spouse is caught in adultery, you can divorce them."

"Preacher?" one of the men said, and just looked at me.

I had to do some deep soul searching in that moment, and they waited, as I looked deep inside myself. Then, I knew what I would do. "No, I wouldn't divorce her," I said. "I would be angry and hurt, but I couldn't divorce her. I love her." And they were satisfied with that answer.

I wasn't just saying that for their sake. I was remembering something that had happened to us when I was still stationed at Ft. Carson. We had gotten into a heated argument in our room, and Pearly threatened to go home. I said to her, "Well, go on home, then." She decided she would take me up on it, so she got her things together, and I accommodated her by taking her to the bus station and letting her out.

Then it settled over me what was happening. My wife, the woman I had committed to spend the rest of my life with, was leaving me. I went inside the station and began to reason with her. My emotions began erupting to the surface, and I couldn't contain the tears. I rushed outside again to hide them, but the more I tried to hide my tears, the worse it got. I was surprised at how much I loved that woman and how desperately I wanted her to be with me.

In reality, I don't think Pearly intended to leave me permanently. She was expecting our first child, and it was

The Commander's anointing

customary for women to go home to deliver. Still, I was shaken by the experience and didn't ever want to lose her.

The Elders' Council was satisfied that day, and I was ordained an elder in the church.

> I WAS SURPRISED AT HOW MUCH I LOVED THAT WOMAN AND HOW DESPERATELY I WANTED HER TO BE WITH ME!

Brother DeLette Also Recognized My Anointing

Brother DeLette was another man who recognized my anointing. After we met, for the next eight years, we stay connected. We would go to his meetings, and he would come to minister to us.

Under his tent one night, he was preaching about Elijah and Elisha. He turned to me and said, "Follow me." I got behind him and literally began following him around the tent as he preached and ministered.

Sometimes, he would make a sharp turn, to test me, and I would have to follow. I was able to stay right with him.

What was he doing? Something was being imparted to me that night. He wasn't just having me follow him around

The Seeds Mature

through the aisles of the tent. He wanted me to take up his mantle. Within a few years he would be gone from this earth, and I would find myself doing many of the same things he had done.

Just a few months before he left us, he told us that his time here was very short. Then a sister received great courage and spoke out something she did not want to speak, that God would soon take him. "The Lord says," she told him, "that you should lay your hands on Pastor Gaddie and impart to him your anointing." He did this.

The last time we were with Brother DeLette, Pearly and I flew to Knoxville, Tennessee, at his request. He had some contacts he wanted to set us up with. He left there and went to Virginia, where he was to do a Shareathon on television, and we went on to Lexington, Kentucky. On his way back home, he experienced an aneurysm and a stroke. He severely damaged his vehicle, and yet he was able to drive it home. At seventy-nine, he was still as tough as nails.

He had been with us in November and had celebrated his birthday with us, and I fully meant to have him back that summer. But it was not to be. We did have him in January, but that was the last time. When we got home from Lexington, there was a message from his son on our answering machine saying that his dad had gone on to be with the Lord. I wept bitterly at the passing of this man, for he meant the world to me.

To some, this relationship might seem strange. G.W. DeLette was a white man, and I'm a black man. But that had nothing to do with it. Or, looking at it in another

The Commander's anointing

way, that difference made it all the more wonderful and miraculous.

God was using His people to prepare me for the future. This man was always concerned about how I was doing, and rarely a day passed without him calling to check on us. In the fall of 2005, when I thought I was dying, he called, sensing that I was not well. He prayed with me on the phone and believed God for my healing. Needless to say, I miss that great man of God.

Pulling Back Periodically

Very early in my Christian experience, the Lord spoke to me and said, "I put you in a league with Moses and Elijah." For many years, I couldn't understand what He was saying. Now I understand that He was trying to tell me, way back then, about the commander's anointing He wanted to place on my life. At the time, however, his words left me mystified. I also saw visions in which I was being greatly used by God.

As we began taking steps of ministry, I felt that I was ready for the anointing I had seen in those visions to come over my life immediately, and I was very disappointed when it didn't happen. Over the coming years, as what the Lord had told me didn't immediately come to pass, I would get discouraged and pull back for a time.

While we were still in Wrightsville, the Lord gave me a vision. I saw myself walking out of a church, and I could tell that I was discouraged.

A woman called out, "Peter."

The Seeds Mature

I turned to face her. "Who are you talking to?" I asked.

"The Lord wants to speak to you," she said.

The moment she said that, my legs folded back in the air, and I went hurtling toward the north wall of the building, my hands elevated. The wall disappeared, and there was an open sky.

Then rain began to fall on me, but it wasn't wet. This rain was fire, and it came from the presence of the Lord. A white-hot ball of fire also came forth from the presence of the Lord. It hit my arm and went down into my body.

Then, the vision changed, and suddenly, I stood before multitudes of people. They were like blades of grass in a lawn, impossible to number. I saw myself ministering to them, and God was doing great miracles.

Down through the years, God blessed me to a certain degree, but when His blessings did not reach to the extent He had shown me, I got upset and pulled back. I knew what I had seen, and I wanted to experience nothing less than that. During those times, I would sit back like a sulking child in protest. Why God tolerated me I'm not sure.

I was like some pouting potentate. God wasn't doing things to my satisfaction, so I sat back, frustrated and angry. "God's going to slap the fire out of you," Pearly warned me one day. As usual, her words were prophetic.

My Katrina Experience

Everything suddenly came to a head in August of 2005, just before the infamous Katrina slammed into the Gulf

The Commander's anointing

Coast. One morning I found that I suddenly could not walk right, and just as suddenly, I lost my appetite. Within a very short time, I had lost thirty pounds. My whole body trembled, and my short-term memory began to fail. When some of my faithful members visited me, I chastised them for not coming earlier. "We were here, Pastor, they protested." I couldn't remember their visit.

While I was in this terrible physical and mental state, the enemy attacked me as never before. "You didn't obey God," he taunted, and he reminded me of specific things I had failed to do through the years. "Now, you're cut off," he concluded, and I was terrified that he was right.

He came into my room and touched my feet, reminding me constantly of his presence and his power over me. At one point, he even went under me. My power of reason came and went over a period of thirty days, and the mental torment of it was unbearable.

Sister Pearly took me to the Veteran's Administration Hospital to get a CAT Scan, an MRI and to have blood work done. My hands shook constantly. Oddly, the VA doctors couldn't find anything wrong with me.

While I was going through all of that, the Lord gave me a dream. I wanted so badly to write down what I had seen, and I started to do. But, when an hour had passed, and I had only a few sentences written down and was exhausted, I called Pearly and asked if she would write down the rest. I didn't want to forget it, and I couldn't write it myself. I told her the dream, and she wrote it down.

The Seeds Mature

One night, in the middle of the night, I fell out of bed, and she was unable to get me back into it. There was no one there to help her, and she didn't know what to do. Finally, using her own weight to leverage me, she dragged me out of our bedroom and down the hallway to another bedroom, where she hoped to get me into a lower bed.

By the time she got me near the bed, her strength was waning. "Help me," she cried. I exerted all the strength I could, and together we wrestled my body onto the bed.

She was afraid to leave me alone the next morning to go to her work, so she called a deacon to come and sit with me all day. He didn't go home until very late that night.

> **EVERYTHING SUDDENLY CAME TO A HEAD IN AUGUST OF 2005!**

"Get Up"

The next night I woke up, and something had changed. Without thinking about what I was doing, I sat up and threw my legs over the side of the bed. I sat there for a while, and then the Spirit of the Lord spoke to me and said, "Get up!"

"I can't get up," I protested in my mind. "I'll fall."

I sat there for the longest time, pondering what I was sure I had heard the Lord say and wondering how I could do it.

The Commander's anointing

If the Lord said it, I began thinking, *then I should be able to do it.* The more I thought about it, the more sure I was that He *had* said it and that I *could* do it. So I tried. Pushing myself out of the bed, I got up, and I started to walk. And I *could* walk. I walked through the whole house.

I was so excited that I woke Sister Gaddie up, and we rejoiced together. From that point on, my health began to improve.

"If Ye Forgive"

The first time I went back to church, I was still very weak, but I wanted to share that experience with the people. Saints stood beside me and behind me to keep me upright, and I barely had enough strength to hold the microphone, but I was able to tell them what had happened to me.

That day, God took me back twenty years to something that someone had done against me and allowed me to forgive them. All that time, I had refused to let it go. It was buried deep inside my mind, and the Lord had to pull it to the surface, so that it could be dealt with. Jesus said:

> *For if ye forgive men their trespasses, your heavenly Father will also forgive you: but if ye forgive not men their trespasses, neither will your Father forgive your trespasses.*   Matthew 6:14-15

Our church was full that day, and the people later said that the anointing was powerful. The Lord let me see that no matter what people do, we have to forgive them. We're not doing it for their sake, but for our own. If we don't forgive others, then God can't forgive us. Our people were greatly blessed by this revelation.

Regaining Strength

After that, we went out of town. Sister Gaddie had a meeting in Holly Springs, Mississippi, and she refused to leave me behind. I was recovering, but I still had a long way to go. She didn't want something to happen to me while she was gone, and Hurricane Rita was on its way toward Houston.

By the time we arrived in Memphis, we saw on the news that the residents of Houston were strung out all the way to Dallas, bumper to bumper. She was so glad she hadn't left me. "You would have been trying to get everyone out, and it would have killed you," she said.

Every night of those meetings, I would get up and say a few words before she got up to preach, and each night I got a little stronger. When I had left home, I was still as weak as a baby, but by the time I got back home, I was as strong as a lion. My people were amazed to see the rapid progress I had made.

It was while we were there in Holly Springs that God began to speak to me the message of *The Commander's Anointing*. We were unable to travel back together because the flight was over-booked, and I had to go by way of Detroit. While I was waiting there in Detroit, the Lord

The Commander's anointing

continued to speak to me and show me more about this high level of anointing. Since then, the revelation has been continual.

> BY THE TIME I GOT BACK HOME, I WAS AS STRONG AS A LION!

The Relationship with Moses

Now I understand my relationship with Moses. As a young man, he had tried to deliver the children of Israel from slavery by killing an Egyptian man. That hadn't worked, and he had then been forced to flee to the desert and to stay there for many years. It was only after his experience at the burning bush that he was able to start doing what God had placed in his heart years before to do. From that point on, Moses had another forty years of fruitful ministry. I sensed that a new day was dawning for me too, and I rejoiced.

In recent months, as I've continued to ponder the goodness of God, His Word has taken on a whole new life to me. As I read of the prophets and kings of old, suddenly what I'm reading is illuminated, and it leaps off of the page into my heart. Not only do I understand what happened to *them*, but I also understand its relationship to *me* and what God

The Seeds Mature

has called *me* to do in the days ahead. Every miracle of the Bible now has a new meaning.

I'm ready to enter every door the Lord opens and to do all that He has prepared me to do. Even now, many new and exciting miracles are taking place in my ministry, and I know it's only the beginning.

Over the years, I've seen every imaginable miracle, but only in a measure of what God has promised me. For instance, one of my son's ears was blown out when he had some boys jump on him. A doctor examined it and said that they would have to do surgery and apply a "screen" to that ear. We prayed, and God fully restored his hearing.

I've seen the multiplication of food. I've seen God do many financial miracles. Now all of that will be multiplied many times over.

A Dream

Not long ago, God gave me a dream that deeply disturbed me. I knew it had a meaning, but I couldn't understand what that meaning was.

In the dream, I saw a German officer, but he was also a wolf. Then there were two of them, both in uniform, and they were going up and down, by turn, the guide wire on a telephone pole. Their movements were smooth, almost choreographed.

Then I saw several more of them standing to one side, watching what was happening. I felt rather uneasy about

The Commander's anointing

them, but since I was at some distance from them, it seemed that I could watch and not be harmed. Gradually, a crowd gathered to see what was happening.

The next time I looked, I was stretched out in the air, and one of the wolves that had been going up and down on the guide wire said to the one who looked like a German officer, "Can I have my way with him? Can I do what I want to do with him?" It was in that moment that I woke up.

I immediately went and told Sister Gaddie about the dream, but she also wasn't sure what it could mean. Next, I called our daughter Lisa. We often call her Josephine because, like Joseph of old, she has a gift of dreaming and interpreting dreams. This particular day, she didn't have anything to say about it, but she promised to call me the moment she did. In the meantime, my spirit remained troubled.

That evening, she called back to say that she had the answer. Just as a spirit was loosed among the Germans that caused them to attempt to annihilate a race of people, I had to be on my guard against a spirit that had been loosed against me. I could no longer just take things for granted. Too much was at stake.

In the past, when things had not gone the way I thought they should, I would cool off and hang back. Now I could not afford to do that. I could not be caught in a state of spiritual repose. I had to stay on guard at all times. Alertness and vigilance were now called for, as, more than ever, the adversary was lurking to do whatever harm he could. Peter had warned the Church of this very thing:

The Seeds Mature

Be sober, be vigilant; because your adversary the devil, as a roaring lion, walketh about, seeking whom he may devour: Whom resist stedfast in the faith. 1 Peter 5:8-9

The enemy, of course, is not about to give up. Anytime we are making progress in God, we become a threat to his kingdom. Now, I would have to stay on top spiritually at all times. I couldn't afford to become discouraged at any moment. These were critical times, and I must remain focused.

All of this is nothing new to most of us, and we should always do it, but for me, it now has added meaning. The Lord has allowed me to see the seriousness of it and what is at stake if we fail.

Because of where I am spiritually and what God is doing through me, the enemy has upped the ante on my life. Every day I must consecrate myself more and seek God more. Many of the things I have gone through were just part of my formation.

Going Back to Little Rock

I would soon be going back to Little Rock for a city-wide revival, and I was expecting great things. God had spoken to me many years before and said:

And they that shall be of thee shall build the old waste places: thou shalt raise up the foundations of many generations; and thou shalt be called, The repairer of the breach, The restorer of paths to dwell in. Isaiah 58:12

The Commander's anointing

Now it was time for the fulfillment of this promise, and I knew that I would see souls saved, people healed and saints restored. I was expecting God to do great miracles.

God's Patience

God has been so very patient with me. At times, I was extremely impatient with the pace of things and became angry with God that He wasn't doing what He had promised me. In reality, God had to deal with immaturity in me. And He has done that. My personal Katrina brought me to my senses and got me on track to do the will of God.

I have seen many ministers rise quickly, only to fall, because of pride and its accompanying temptations. With some, it was alcohol. With others, it was women or money. I'm glad for what I've suffered, and I know that I'm not above being tempted, but I understand the depth of what is at stake, and I now say to the devil, "Don't even try it with me." I know too much.

Now, I'm ready for my future, and it's here.

Chapter 9

The Commander's Anointing Today

For ye see your calling, brethren, how that not many wise men after the flesh, not many mighty, not many noble, are called: But God hath chosen the foolish things of the world to confound the wise; and God hath chosen the weak things of the world to confound the things which are mighty; and base things of the world, and things which are despised, hath God chosen, yea, and things which are not, to bring to nought things that are: that no flesh should glory in his presence. 1 Corinthians 1:26-29

God is not against knowledge or wisdom, but He always wants to receive the glory. Because of that, He often raises up the most unlikely candidates to do His bidding.

The Commander's anointing

God Chooses Unlikely Candidates

When He works through any individual, God's not doing it for the sake of pumping up someone's pride, to make him or her feel good about themselves. He alone deserves all the glory.

> **GOD OFTEN RAISES UP THE MOST UNLIKELY CANDIDATES TO DO HIS BIDDING!**

When God chooses us, we often feel unworthy. In fact, of all the men and women who were called in Bible days, not one of them felt adequate for the task at hand. To the contrary, like us, they usually felt totally inadequate. Moses, for example, was sure that he couldn't even talk right, and he complained so much about it that God was angered and ordained his brother Aaron to be his public spokesman:

And he shall be thy spokesman unto the people: and he shall be, even he shall be to thee instead of a mouth, and thou shalt be to him instead of God.   Exodus 4:16

Once Moses began seeing God's power at work in his life, his courage level rose, and he no longer had any difficulty speaking.

The Commander's Anointing Today

Even the apostle Paul, with all his wisdom and knowledge, recognized that his power and authority were not a result of it. He said:

> *But what things were gain to me, those I counted loss for Christ. Yea doubtless, and I count all things but loss for the excellency of the knowledge of Christ Jesus my Lord: for whom I have suffered the loss of all things, and do count them but dung, that I may win Christ, and be found in him, not having mine own righteousness, which is of the law, but that which is through the faith of Christ, the righteousness which is of God by faith.*
>
> Philippians 3:7-9

"The excellency of the knowledge of Christ" is so much more valuable than all other knowledge that Paul pushed the rest to the side so that he could win Christ.

When we're working for God, our own intellect can often get in the way. If we're going to do His work, then we have to do it *His* way. It's when we surrender to the Lord, lay aside our preconceived ideas about how things should be done, and let Him stand at the forefront, that His blessings begin to come to us, and then, through us, to others.

Believe me, with every step I've taken in God, I've been so afraid that the Lord has had to comfort me. Many times, when telling people how nervous I've been at various points in my journey, they found it hard to believe. But it was only too true. Confidence comes from walking with the Lord. In our natural state, we are incompetent to fulfill His dictates.

The Commander's anointing

Crowds have always made me nervous, but when the Lord has me by the hand, I can face any crowd. Our confidence is in the Lord, not in ourselves.

The men and women who have carried the commander's anointing down through history didn't necessarily think much of themselves, but God honored them anyway. That's just the way He does it.

We Have Everything that Has Gone Before — Plus

The commander's anointing was seen in the prophets, the judges and the kings. It worked in Gideon, Joshua and Moses and then Jesus and the disciples. We have now come to the end, and we have everything that has gone before, plus what Jesus left us, plus the new anointing for our own time.

Because we are now in the time of the end, we can inherit everything that has gone before. Everything these men and women had is available to us—and more. It's a new day. Because of this, there's nothing that we cannot do in this hour. Literally nothing!

On one of our trips home from Philadelphia, Sister Gaddie prayed, "Lord, give us Godspeed." I can't say for sure what happened, but I do know this: somehow and some way, we got a day ahead of ourselves. It reminded me of what happened the night Jesus came to His disciples walking on the sea:

The Commander's Anointing Today

So when they had rowed about five and twenty or thirty furlongs, they see Jesus walking on the sea, and drawing nigh unto the ship: and they were afraid. But he saith unto them, It is I; be not afraid. Then they willingly received him into the ship: and immediately the ship was at the land whither they went. John 6:19-21

When the storm had arisen, they were in the midst, or the middle, of the sea. But, once Jesus got on board, they were *"immediately ... at the land."* Now that's a miracle. And if God did it then, He can do it again.

What happened with all the territory in between the middle of the sea and the land? Who's to say? The important thing to remember is that Jesus could do these miracles, and He is within us, so can we do them too. God is God, and He can do anything He wants to do. And, because He is our God, we can do the undoable.

The question was asked of Abraham:

Is any thing too hard for the LORD? Genesis 18:14

The answer, of course, was that there was nothing too hard for Him. And, since God has not changed and is just the same today, it is still true. Nothing is too hard for God. And, since we are His ambassadors in the earth, nothing is too hard for us.

On several occasions, I've given away the last bills I had in my billfold, only to find more money there later. God has also multiplied the money in our bank account. We've gone through a lot of very tight times, but God has always been there to provide our needs.

The commander's anointing was demonstrated periodically down through history. Sometimes hundreds of years passed with no one exhibiting this gift, and sometimes it was even thousands of years. But when this authority was again in demonstration, the person who received it received all that the former commanders had received, plus something new. Therefore, the commander's anointing in our time will be greater than at any other time in history. The men or women who totally surrender themselves to God will lay hold of it, and great things will be accomplished in a short space of time.

It's So Important to Walk in Humility and Seek God's Wisdom

Because of this, it's so important that we walk in humility. What has been given to you can just as quickly and easily be taken away from you—if you fail to walk in humility before God and man. This is one of the things that have hurt many ministries.

Wisdom is available to us, if we will just seek it. When Solomon was thrust into a role he felt unqualified for, he prayed for wisdom, and God told him it was already done:

> *Behold, I have done according to thy words: lo, I have given thee a wise and an understanding heart; so that there*

The Commander's Anointing Today

was none like thee before thee, neither after thee shall any arise like unto thee.   1 Kings 3:12

Solomon probably didn't feel any different in that moment, but God said that wisdom was now present in his life, so it was there—regardless of how Solomon felt.

He had been thrust into that role, and now God was giving him wisdom to do what he was called to do.

Today, with the responsibility of the fivefold ministry upon us, we often feel our lack of wisdom. But all we have to do is ask, and God said He would give it to us:

> *If any of you lack wisdom, let him ask of God, that giveth to all men liberally, and upbraideth not; and it shall be given him.* James 1:5

IT'S SO IMPORTANT THAT WE WALK IN HUMILITY!

That doesn't mean that we have no need to study God's Word or pray, but it means that suddenly something is unlocked in our understanding, and we know what to do and how to do it, and we don't know how we know it.

Recently, I am rereading portions of scripture that I have read many times through the years, and suddenly new meaning is popping out at me, feeding my soul.

It's possible to read the Scriptures and it's just that: reading. Then, suddenly, God begins to open our understanding to it, and that's something entirely different.

The Commander's anointing

It's Time for Revelation

When I was still very young in the Lord (in my early thirties), I had an unusual experience that showed me what God wanted to do with my life. I was walking along listening to a sermon on the radio. The man who was preaching that day had some definite revelation on the subject, but at the same time I was listening to him, I began receiving some very different, but deep, revelation of my own on the passage under consideration. The man was showing me some things, but God was showing me more. And that's what He wants to do for every one of us.

When God begins to open our understanding, that's the beginning of a new level of authority in our lives. That's the beginning of the commander's anointing being released in us. If we are to lead others into new truths and experiences, we must first have those truths and experiences ourselves.

It's Time for this Anointing

Jesus was a great commander long before He appeared in Bethlehem's manger, but in due time, God sent Him to the earth. The people desperately needed Him. Again, today, there is a great need for deliverance in the land. We desperately need the presence of the Lord to show up and permeate our areas of battle.

Our world has given itself up to all sorts of perversion, causing even Sodom and Gomorrah to blush. Today people

The Commander's Anointing Today

are blatant about their sin. They no longer hide it in shame. Rather, they proudly parade their evil deeds before us all and dare us to challenge their morality. Yet, in the midst of such perversions, God has a Man who will stand with us, as we face every impending battle. His Word declares:

> *Cry aloud, spare not, lift up thy voice like a trumpet, and show my people their transgression, and the house of Jacob their sins.*   Isaiah 58:1

That command is to you and me. It's up to us now.

Too many churches have compromised and now preach only a social gospel. They make the people who attend their services feel good, but, as God's servants, we are called to say what He says. Not many have the courage to do that today. In the days ahead, some of us will actually seal our testimony with blood. Nevertheless, we cannot afford to compromise. We have a mandate from Heaven, and we must be faithful to that mandate—regardless of the cost.

Martyrdom at Columbine

Several weeks before Columbine and the other infamous school shootings began here in this country, God gave me a vision, and I spoke about it to my people. "The children of America are about to get themselves into something their parents can't get them out of," I said, and a couple of weeks later, it all started.

At Columbine, one young lady, who had been shot and wounded, was overheard by the shooters to be praying to

The Commander's anointing

God. "Well," one of the shooters said, "since you believe in God, let me just send you where He is." And, with that, he shot her again, this time at close range, and she died. That God-hating spirit is growing in the world, and we will see more of that type of thing in the near future.

When Peter asked Jesus about the future of John, Jesus had an interesting answer:

> **GET READY FOR WHATEVER COMES YOUR WAY!**

> *Then Peter, turning about, seeth the disciple whom Jesus loved following; which also leaned on his breast at supper, and said, Lord, which is he that betrayeth thee? Peter seeing him saith to Jesus, Lord, and what shall this man do? Jesus saith unto him, If I will that he tarry till I come, what is that to thee? follow thou me.*
>
> John 21:20-22

Make up your mind to follow the Lord unto death—no matter what others do. He said:

> *Fear none of those things which thou shalt suffer: behold, the devil shall cast some of you into prison, that ye may be tried; and ye shall have tribulation ten days: be thou faithful unto death, and I will give thee a crown of life.*
>
> Revelation 2:10

The Commander's Anointing Today

Get ready for whatever comes your way.

This World Has Nothing to Offer

I have drunk deeply from the cup of this world, so I know it has nothing to offer me. I've had material things, and I know they can't satisfy. I can say, without reservation, that sex and alcohol are not the panaceas they are cracked up to be. I've been there, and I know what I'm talking about. After all I've been through, I'm blessed to still be alive, but I'm alive for a purpose. God has spared me to do His will, and that's what my life is all about now.

I understand that most people, especially young people who have not lived long yet, find it difficult to believe us when we say that this world holds nothing for us. In their stubbornness, they will insist on finding out for themselves, and what can we say? Some people have to learn everything the hard way.

A Healing Ministry

God has healed me many times. I've had cancer, heart attacks and strokes, and He's always raised me up. I could write a book just on my healings. At least three times in my life, I've been unable to walk on my own, and God miraculously healed me. The last time, as I noted in an earlier chapter, He just said, "Get up," and my healing began. Now I carry a healing ministry. I've been ministering healing to some extent through the years, but the healing anointing has now increased upon my life.

As for myself, I am in the hands of God. At one point, I went to the hospital for a checkup, and the doctor determined that I was in perfectly good health. Then, suddenly, my heart began to fail. I felt like I was running out of gas. The Lord spoke to my spirit and said, "Your life is in my hands." So, from now on, it doesn't really matter what doctors say. They have nothing to do with it. I know that I'm not going anywhere until God is ready for me to go. That doesn't mean that I plan to do something crazy. It just means that I know that God is in control of my life.

Cling to What Is Precious

We must cling to things that are truly precious. A church in southern Arkansas purchased a piece of property and prepared to build on it. After the land was inspected, they were told that it was not suitable for building and that they could not, therefore, put up their proposed building. Then, mysteriously, God told the church leaders to build anyway, and they started.

When their building activity reached the attention of the local inspectors, they came to see what was happening. "Didn't we tell you that you couldn't build on this site?" they demanded.

"You did," the pastor told them, "but God told us to go ahead. Please check the soil again." Reluctantly, the inspectors did their tests again and, this time, they found, to their amazement, that the consistency of the soil had changed. Every spot they drilled was now suitable for building.

I went to visit that place, and I brought back with me a bag of that soil. It's a constant reminder to me of God's power. Some might wonder what I wanted with a bag of dirt. Isn't dirt just dirt? Well, there's dirt and then there's *this* dirt. This is special dirt. God Himself put it in that place, and it's a testimony to His great power. In the days ahead, we must cling to that which is precious and hold lightly that which is little more than passing fancy.

Be Careful

Be careful. Some see others doing the work of God, and they say to themselves, "I can do that," but that's dangerous. God doesn't want anyone involved in His work who thinks they can do it. They can't; only He can do it.

There is no room for puffed-up flesh in God's Church. He can't stand pride. He said:

> *That your faith should not stand in the wisdom of men, but in the power of God. Howbeit we speak wisdom among them that are perfect: yet not the wisdom of this world, nor of the princes of this world, that come to nought: but we speak the wisdom of God in a mystery, even the hidden wisdom, which God ordained before the world unto our glory.* 1 Corinthians 2:5-7

The Commander's anointing

The apostle Paul was privileged to study with the great Jewish teacher Gamaliel, and yet he counted it all as dung so that he could glorify Christ. It's not about being born in the right family, possessing the right pedigree and the right education. It's all in the call from God, and when He calls a man or woman, He qualifies them for His work, placing upon their lives the commander's anointing.

When the late great Ruth Heflin was considering where she should study for the ministry, God spoke to her to trust Him to prepare her instead. She had considered attending Wheaton College, as her famous Uncle William A. Ward had, but God said that if she would stay before Him, He would give her His wisdom. Ruth obeyed God and went on to touch every nation of the world for Him before her untimely death at the age of sixty. How could anyone outdo what God does?

Jesus was not born in a palace, but in a stable, and what did people expect to come forth from a humble stable? His parents chose to raise Him in Nazareth, and the question was later asked, "Can there any good thing come out of Nazareth?"

> And Nathanael said unto him [Philip], Can there any good thing come out of Nazareth? Philip saith unto him, Come and see.　　　　　　　　　　　John 1:46

The Son of God did not come into this world with a silver spoon in His mouth. He was a man of low degree, but that didn't stop Him from doing mighty works. And, through it, God the Father received all the glory.

The Commander's Anointing Today

When Jesus was found in the Temple in Jerusalem at the age of twelve, discussing things in an intelligent way with the doctors of the law, it "blew their minds." How did such a young lad have so much wisdom?

Still, as great as He was, Jesus choose to make Himself *"of no reputation,"* and we are to emulate His life:

> *Let this mind be in you, which was also in Christ Jesus: who, being in the form of God, thought it not robbery to be equal with God: but made himself of no reputation, and took upon him the form of a servant, and was made in the likeness of men: and being found in fashion as a man, he humbled himself, and became obedient unto death, even the death of the cross. Wherefore God also hath highly exalted him, and given him a name which is above every name: that at the name of Jesus every knee should bow, of things in heaven, and things in earth, and things under the earth; and that every tongue should confess that Jesus Christ is Lord, to the glory of God the Father.*
>
> Philippians 2:5-11

> **WHEN GOD CALLS A MAN OR WOMAN, HE QUALIFIES THEM FOR HIS WORK!**

Jesus knew where He had come from, and He knew where He was going. How about you?

The Commander's anointing

The men who got behind David and made him a success were running away from Saul. They were so dedicated to David that they fought until their hands were weary from holding the sword, and then they kept on fighting. In the end, they became great because David, their leader, was great. When he became king, they were known as *"David's mighty men."* They had started out as a rag-tag group of misfits, disgruntled and disgraced, but identifying themselves with David and his commander's anointing made them great.

It's Time for Obedience

The Lord gave me a dream. I went to a hair salon that was located in someone's home. When I went in, I looked around. The hairdressers were busy with customers, but there was a man seated on a couch in a waiting area. The Spirit said to me, "Pray for him." I didn't feel anything special, but then I know that when God speaks, it's not necessary to feel anything special. I began to pray for the man, and the power of God fell on him, and he began speaking in other tongues. He hadn't even been saved, and this wonderful thing happened. The dream made me realize that through the years I have suffered a lot of loss because I've not been more obedient to God in such things.

When I was young, I went into a doctor's office one day, to find it full of sick people. I felt impressed to pray for a certain lady there, but I was hesitant to do it right there in front of everyone. I did speak with her. I asked her where

The Commander's Anointing Today

she lived and what her problem was, and I even promised that I would visit her and pray for her. But that's not what God had told me to do. The anointing was present in that moment to heal, and I missed the opportunity. I felt it lift and realized my mistake, but it was too late to do anything about it. I did learn a lesson that day. Nothing is more important than obedience to God. When working for Him, we're dealing with His Church, His Word and His people. We must do things *His* way.

When God moves on you to do something, do it. If He tells you to do it tomorrow, that's fine, but if He tells you to do it today, tomorrow will be too late. If I had obeyed God that day, the healing of that one woman could have led to the healing of others, and we might have emptied out the whole office full of sick people. Don't miss your opportunity to act.

Chapter 10

What Lies Ahead?

But call to remembrance the former days.
                              Hebrews 10:32

Several years ago I went back to that rural area south of Little Rock where we had lived back in the 1950s, and I took a little trip down memory lane. It was very fruitful.

Our House Was Gone

Our house had sat in the curve of the main road leading north and south, and all night long, the sound of trucks gearing up and down could be heard. We were so accustomed to it that it was music to our ears.

The Commander's anointing

Just in front of us was a railroad track, and trains came by there regularly. The mail bag from the local postal service was attached to a pole near the tracks, and when the train came by, it snagged the bag and took the outgoing mail with it.

Also nearby was an area where railroad cars were loaded with gravel and sand for shipment to other cities. A large wooden ramp had been constructed out of creosoted wooden beams, and dump trucks backed onto the ramp and dumped their loads directly into the rail cars. Once the cars were full, an engine pulled them away. We watched this operation with endless fascination. Those sounds were like lullabies to us as children.

Our little house had a tin roof, and when it would rain, the sound of the rain on that roof would put us into a deep sleep.

Not far away, down in the bottom, was a large field where Mr. Radcliff grew cotton. We children often picked cotton in that field to earn extra money for the family. Mr. Radcliff's big house sat up on the hill. That house is still standing, and his wife is also still living.

The Radcliffs had horses and they also raised Hereford cattle. Each spring, they had new colts and new calves. It was fascinating seeing them in the fields.

The house we had lived in, the big tree beside it and many of the neighboring houses were all gone, but they were not gone from my mind. The railroad tracks were still there, and I walked them until I could identify the spot where the house had once stood.

What Lies Ahead?

I stood there for a while, and memories flooded my soul. Since I had no one else to talk to, I had a little talk with my guardian angel that day:

You haven't changed, but I have. I've changed a lot.
You've been around for a long time now. You were there watching over me when I was just a small baby and you stayed with me as I grew up. You know all about the struggles and the tests. And you know the purpose they served. You knew it long before I did.
All the houses that were here are gone, but I know that you remember it all. I certainly do. I'll never forget it. In this place, the seeds were sown for my life as it is today and as it will be tomorrow. And I'm grateful.
I didn't always understand it, but now I do.

THE HOUSE WE HAD LIVED IN, THE BIG TREE BESIDE IT AND MANY OF THE NEIGHBORING HOUSES WERE ALL GONE!

It was an extremely nostalgic moment.

The Commander's anointing

The Blot of Racism

As I stood there, I couldn't help remembering Mr. Pott's plot of rabbit grass. That grass was so sweet (with a little tinge of sour), and we loved to pick it for his rabbits and taste some of it ourselves. I don't know where you can find any of that grass today. I haven't seen it in years.

Mr. Potts was a white man, and we grew up playing with his children, so we knew nothing of racial prejudice in our immediate neighborhood. It wasn't until I had gone into other areas of town that we saw what prejudice was. And it was only after I had left Arkansas and was in other places for my military training that I was treated badly because of the color of my skin. I wondered what was wrong with people who were acting that way. I'd never seen such an attitude in my life.

When most people think of Arkansas, they think of racial injustice, but, for the most part, our state was not a place of racial division. My children also grew up knowing nothing of prejudice. It was only in 1977, when they first saw the television mini-series *Roots*, made from Alex Haley's famous book of that same name, that they became aware of its terrible effects. They were horrified. They had known nothing of the things previous generations had suffered.

God's Not With Us in Our Prejudices

In recent years, the Lord has done much to elevate the Black race, and He has done the same for women. Both of

What Lies Ahead?

us now have a greater platform than ever. But there are still people around who will not accept Black ministers and others who will not accept women in this role.

When our son went to be with the Lord, we chose a woman to preach his funeral. That angered the pastor of the church we used. Many churches in Houston had offered to accommodate the homegoing service, but we chose that particular church because it was closer to us and more convenient to our people. The pastor later sent me word that if he had known we were going to allow a woman to preach, he wouldn't have let us use the church. Well, if I had known he was so against women preachers, I would never have asked to use his church in the first place.

I've grown to the place in God that I see very clearly that He is simply not with us in our prejudices. Those who are still against women preachers and those who still judge a man by the color of his skin need to grow up. Those are vestiges of a bygone era, and this is a new day.

It's a New Day

Today, God is revealing Himself to us in a new way. Beginning with Abraham, as God chose to deal with men and women, He revealed more of Himself to them. When he spoke to Abraham, it was for himself, his seed and the nation to come. And then, with each succeeding generation, He revealed another part of Himself.

For example, when Abraham was called upon to sacrifice Isaac, and he proved faithful, suddenly a ram was

The Commander's anointing

revealed caught in the bushes, and God showed Abraham that the ram was to be the sacrifice to replace Isaac. In this way, God showed Himself as Jehovah Jireh, God who Provides, and no one before that day had known Him in that particular way.

When Abraham went out to fight against the kings who had kidnapped Lot and his family, God revealed Himself in yet another way, as Abraham's shield and reward. The people lived in the open in tents in those days, and God wanted them to know that He would protect them. He was all they needed:

> **GOD REVEALED HIMSELF IN YET ANOTHER WAY, AS ABRAHAM'S SHIELD AND REWARD!**

After these things the word of the LORD came unto Abram in a vision, saying, Fear not, Abram: I am thy shield, and thy exceeding great reward.   Genesis 15:1

Jesus would later promise in the New Testament:

Lo, I am with you alway, even unto the end of the world. Amen.   Matthew 28:20

This promise gives us great security. We can lie down and sleep, without having to keep one eye open.

What Lies Ahead?

The Sorrows of the Past Serve a Positive Purpose

Surprisingly, as I stood there that day pondering the meaning of all that we had experienced as children, my memories were, for the most part, pleasant ones. Even the sorrows of life seemed to serve a useful purpose.

Not long ago, I saw a reenactment of *The Trail of Tears* performed in a church. When it was finished, there was not a dry eye in the place, and the altars were filled with repentant men and women, boys and girls.

It was very sad the way the Native American people were treated. That all happened a long time ago, but with God, yesterday is right now. Tomorrow, today and yesterday are the same to Him, and He allowed me to sense the pain and suffering those noble people had endured.

Once most of the bison were killed, it spelled the end of a centuries-old way of life for these noble people. Those great animals represented their very livelihood. They not only ate the meat of the bison; they used its hide to make their clothing and tents.

Slowly, their land was stolen, and they were pushed out to live in places not conducive to their way of life. Now God is using those scenes of destruction and death to bring salvation to many. Thank God for that. Even sorrow bears fruit.

The Commander's anointing

I Pulled Myself Away

It was difficult for me to pull myself away from the place that day. There were so many memories to ponder, so many truths to recognize. And, when I left, it was with both sadness and anticipation. So much of the life we had known growing up as children was gone, never to be recovered again. And yet a new and very exciting life lay ahead. God has great things for all of us. Let us learn from our yesterdays and make our todays and our tomorrows better—for ourselves and for everyone around us. This is our calling, and this is our anointing.

For me to claim such an anointing personally is a great miracle. Many years ago the Lord spoke to me through the words of Isaiah:

> *And therefore will the* Lord *wait, that he may be gracious unto you, and therefore will he be exalted, that he may have mercy upon you: for the* Lord *is a God of judgment: blessed are all they that wait for him.*   Isaiah 30:18

When He first spoke these words to me, I didn't fully understand them. Now I do. God has been so patient with me, suffering my ups and downs until the time was right. And now it's God's time to *"be gracious"* to me. I am *"blessed"* because I have waited for Him, and a new anointing is mine today.

Epilogue

When I think back on what Ms. Nancy Spikes did for me—taking me in and raising me like her own son—I'm so very grateful. She clothed me, fed me and bought my school supplies. I've often said that I eventually want to have a place where I can receive needy children, so that I can return some of that blessing poured out so long ago upon me. When I build such a home, I'm determined to put her name on it. It will be the Nancy Spikes Memorial Home. She was worthy of such an honor. She blessed me, so I want to bless others. Hopefully, I can do it on a much larger scale. That would make me very happy.

Such a venture would not be a contradiction of our faith. Even though time is short, and we know the Lord is coming soon, we are not just to sit around and wait for Him. We must do what we can while we can, and when time as we

The Commander's anointing

know it has ended, then we'll rest. In the meantime, there's work to be done to bring in the great end-time harvest.

As God prospers us, everything that our hands find to do for Him, we intend to do. As the wise Solomon instructed (commanded):

> *Whatsoever thy hand findeth to do, do it with thy might; for there is no work, nor device, nor knowledge, nor wisdom, in the grave, whither thou goest.*
>
> Ecclesiastes 9:10

Because of the many things I suffered as a child, I have never taken life for granted, and I've always appreciated what has been done for me and given to me. I know what it is not to have anything, and I realize that prosperity can be taken from us just as quickly as it comes to us. Keeping these things in mind causes us to be appreciative of the present and prayerful for the future. If things should turn bad, I know that by committing myself to God, I can endure and survive. He will help me go through whatever I have to go through, so we'll win either way. In the Lord, we can't lose.

Ms. Spikes was unable to have children of her own, so all of her life, she had been taking children in and caring for them as if they were her own. She helped other people with their children's needs, buying clothes for them. In my case, she went much further. In later years, I asked her, "What made you want to take me in?"

"I really can't explain it," she said. "There was just something about you that attracted me. When I saw you, I

Epilogue

was thinking to myself, 'If I just had a little boy like that, I would do many things for him.' " And that's the way God opened the door. She needed me, and I needed her, and so we benefited each other.

Mother Spikes was good enough to provide for me as a boy, and then God used me and Pearl to lead her to eternal life in Him. Surprisingly, although she had attended church a great part of her life, she had never known salvation. When she did receive the Lord as her personal Savior, there were things about her life-style she had to change. Her cigarettes were the last thing to go. I was there the night it happened, and I remember it well.

I would take her to the church in Little Rock. One night, many people were around the altar, tarrying to receive the Holy Ghost, and Mother Spikes was among them. She prayed for a while, then, suddenly, she stopped praying. It was apparent that something was bothering her. She headed straight for her pocket book, took out her package of cigarettes and threw them away. Then, with a cleared mind, she went back to prayer and was soon filled with the Holy Ghost. Mother Spikes is now in the presence of God, and I will be forever grateful for her compassion to a young boy.

MINISTRY PAGE

You may contact Apostle and Prophetess Gaddie in the following way:

New Jerusalem Whole Truth Church, Inc.
P.O. Box 11007
Houston, TX 77293

(281) 987-0782

first_shepherd@yahoo.com

www.ingramcontent.com/pod-product-compliance
Lightning Source LLC
Chambersburg PA
CBHW032116090426
42743CB00007B/365